Vicki.
May yo
voice of
in this
Blessings + love,
Patricia

The Heart of the Bridegroom for His Bride

Patricia Ducharm

The Heart of the Bridegroom for His Bride by Patricia Ducharm

Cover Design: Kelsey White

ISBN-13: 978-1502757449

ISBN-10: 1502757443

Dedication

I dedicate this book to my Aunt Sally, who was the first to read the writings the Lord gave me. You have encouraged me for years with your love and compassion. Your knowledge of God's Word and your ability to show me where my writings were in Scripture opened me to being able to receive more from the Holy Spirit. The encouragement I received from you inspired me. The ways in which you expressed appreciation of these writings motivated me to continue writing this book.

You are loved beyond words, and I admire you so much. In you, I see a woman of faith who is grounded in God's Word. Anyone who has been privileged to know you has been blessed by your love, compassion, and joy of the Lord.

Special Thanks

First, I give thanks to the Bridegroom. Without You, there would be no book. I am eternally grateful for Your presence in my life.

I want to thank my precious husband, Mike, who has supported me and helped me during this process. Honey, you have been my sounding board and my rock. I want to thank our son Mark and his wife Kimberly for encouraging me to follow my dream, and for our son Dan and his wife Ann for special help in working on the manuscript and believing that the book should be written. Thank you to my siblings Debbie, Cathy, Bob, and dearly departed Carol. Your love and support is so very important to me.

Debbie Adams, I never would have finished this manuscript without your motivation and support. You have mentored me through this process with godly wisdom.

To my friends Patty, Rudi, Carol, Judy, Chris, Lori, Jan, Shannon, and Mary, I thank you for your prayerful presence in my life, as well as your wisdom and encouragement. You bless me beyond measure.

To my editors, Christina Files and Allison Armerding, you brought out the gold in this book. I am so grateful for your professional skills and the many ways you brought everything together.

To Pastor Ron and Louise, and my New Covenant Christian Church family, you have been so very supportive and loving. Words fail to express my love for you. To Pastor Don at The River in California, your presence carries the very heart of the Father's love.

Introduction

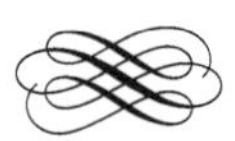

This is my story of how God came for me in love letters, wooing me to Him in healing and in love. The Lord counsels me and draws me out of darkness into the light through meeting me in times of quiet prayer.

This book does not go into the depths of my history, but instead it shows the depths of love the Bridegroom has for His hurting Bride. The Bridegroom does not abandon you, but instead, He searches for you, His Bride, and joins you on the journey out of darkness and into His deep love.

Here is my vision and word of exhortation to you as you read these love letters in the form of devotionals:

You, the bride have taken your first step
down the aisle in your wedding procession

toward your Groom (Jesus). The walk has begun. It matters not how long the walk takes. Do not stop walking toward your Bridegroom. Each time you turn to the Lord is another step forward in the bridal procession. Each choice is a yes to your Groom. Each yes changes who you are eternally. You are not wasting your time, even if you experience nothing emotionally. Walk in faith and your walk will be strengthened. Focus on Him. He is worth the sacrifice. Keep coming.

Taste and see that the Lord is good. The Bridegroom teaches, counsels, corrects and comforts. Hear Him speak of His faithful interest in your life. May you fall more in love with Him. You are His Beloved, and He is yours.

Thus says the Lord, the God of Israel, "Write all the words which I have spoken to you in a book."

Jeremiah 30:2 NASB

Day 1: An Invitation to Friendship

"Greater love has no one than this, than to lay down one's life for his friends...No longer do I call you servants, for a servant does not know what his master is doing; but I have called you friends, for all things that I heard from My Father I have made known to you."
John 15:13, 15

And the Scripture was fulfilled which says, "Abraham believed God, and it was accounted to him for righteousness." And he was called the friend of God.
James 2:23

A man who has friends must himself be friendly,
But there is a friend who sticks closer than a brother.
Proverbs 18:24

My Child,

I call you My Beloved. Do you realize what that means? Beloved means that you are loved and treasured. I hold you near to My heart. Can you receive the love that goes with the name Beloved? Do you hear that you are cherished and named?

You are numbered as My friend. What does it mean to be called My friend? Friends hold an intimate relationship with one another. They are known by each other. There is a degree of trust and value in the relationship. To be known requires revelation. Will you reveal your heart to Me? I already know what your heart contains, but when you reveal it to Me, you are taking a step closer to Me in love. I love to be loved by you. When you reach back to love Me in return, you are releasing part of yourself to Me. Each time you return love to Me, you are growing in your ability to love. I love when you respond to My love for you.

Be established in love, My friend. Rest in the peace of belonging to your Beloved. You have a home to go to. You are safe with Me.

Day 2: Be Attractive in the Spirit

... put on the new man which was created according to God, in true righteousness and holiness.
Ephesians 4:24

For as many of you as were baptized into Christ have put on Christ.
Galatians 3:27

Set your mind on things above, not on things on the earth.
Colossians 3:2

My Dearest,

Not everything depends upon your presentation. What matters most is your heart. That is what you need for adornment—a heart connected to your Lord, a presence that says you have been in the inner throne room of the King.

With My love to adorn you, you will be presentable, however you choose to dress. Your beauty comes from being centered upon your Lord, not from comparing yourself to this person or that person. This is not about how young you look or about how slim you are; it is about *Whose* you are.

You represent Me, so anoint your body with time in My presence. Put My Words upon your lips, and you will be radiant in Me. Focus on the higher things, not the things of this world.

Be in this world but not of it. I will give you what you need. I will be your strength, and I will be your peace. Rest in Me, and you will be at rest. You only need to be yourself to be beautiful. A copy of someone else is only a copy. Be authentic. Be who I have created, and you will shine with a quality that comes only from being you. Do not try to be who you think people want you to be. A poor imitation is deceit, not flattery.

Walk in dignity, My Bride, adorned by My Spirit, and you will stand out as someone rare: "My precious Bride." Do not buy into the ways of the world, as they are shallow. Choose fullness in Me over an exterior with no interior life. Do not go backward, but go forward in the Spirit. I reflect your spiritual beauty.

Day 3: Becoming Spiritually Mature

All Scripture is given by inspiration of God, and is
profitable for doctrine, for reproof, for correction,
for instruction in righteousness,
that the man of God may be complete,
thoroughly equipped for every good work.
2 Timothy 3:16-17

...add to your faith virtue, to virtue knowledge, to
knowledge self-control, to self-control perseverance, to
perseverance godliness...
2 Peter 1:5b-6

Blessed is the man
Who walks not in the counsel of the ungodly,
Nor stands in the path of sinners,
Nor sits in the seat of the scornful;
But his delight is in the law of the LORD,
And in His law he meditates day and night.
He shall be like a tree
Planted by the rivers of water,
That brings forth its fruit in its season,
Whose leaf also shall not wither;
And whatever he does shall prosper.
Psalm 1:1-3

Dearest,

Today is a new day. Write upon it a new message of faithfulness. Press onward toward Me in love and desire. Desire to be pleasing to your Groom. I am calling you to grow up in the Spirit. You are invited to full maturity. What I ask of you is to put aside some of your desires for better choices. What used to fulfill you will no longer do so.

Allow My Word to wash you from the inside out. Sit with My Word and receive it. Do not just read My Word for the sake of doing so. Wake up to My Word. My Word is alive, and I want you to be fully alive in the Spirit. My Word will wake up your spirit, but first it has to be digested. Ponder it before you swallow it. Do not rush the process. Be equipped, as this is your warfare.

Day 4: Being in the Present Moment

"Watch therefore, for you do not know
what hour your Lord is coming."
Matthew 24:42

Then He came to the disciples
and found them sleeping, and said to Peter,
"What! Could you not watch with Me one hour?
Watch and pray, lest you enter into temptation.
The spirit indeed is willing, but the flesh is weak."
Matthew 26:40-41

Draw near to God and He will draw near to you.
Cleanse your hands, you sinners; and purify your
hearts, you double-minded.
James 4:8

Dearest Bride,

Where have you been hiding, My dear one? You have not been listening for My voice. Do you truly long to hear the voice of your Beloved? If so, strain your ears day and night, so I may speak to you. Remember that I am here.

You forget to be prepared for My coming as you busy yourself with your day. You have gotten into a habit of fixing your attention on the tasks before you, or on what has happened in the past, and you are not available in the present moment to hear Me. I am in this very moment. I am not in what just happened, or what will happen. I am in the present moment. Take this moment and be with it, for it is rich in possibilities. This present moment is a gift to you. Come back to Me. Do not listen to the idle chatter in your mind. Come back to Me in the now, over and over again, and I will refresh you.

Find Me in My Word. Speak to Me with My words, and you will be pleasing to Me. I love to hear you say what I say. Remember to say what I say, and not what fear and doubt says. Ponder life, not death. Ponder hope rather than fear. I am hope, and when you are in hope, you are in Me.

Be aware, My dear one, of the many distractions that lead you astray; they have become normal to you, and you do not even recognize them as distractions. Do not be led away by distractions. I know the plans that I have for you, My Bride, and I call you to come closer to Me. Do not run in the opposite direction, but come closer to My heart of love.

Life in the Spirit differs from life in the world. Do not forget to whom you belong, and where your true home is. It is a challenge to be in the world, and not of the world. By coming back to the present moment, you will find a serenity you have not found before. Tell yourself the truth, and you will not be lost. I am the Truth.

Oh, My Bride, I am here. If you only knew how special our times together are, you would not distract yourself from them so automatically. Believe that you are My Bride and act like it, for I have indeed called you by name. You are chosen and betrothed to the One who calls you.

Turn more and more to Me, as I will teach you many things. I love to have your ear and your heart. My heart quickens when you make time for Me, as I am already here waiting for you. Do not keep Me waiting for you, as I long for intimacy with you. This is My promise to you. I will be with you always.

Do not fear. Doubt less and stretch your faith—then you will see how your faith grows. At My feet you will find a banquet of wisdom and love. Where do you choose to sit? How do you choose to be fed—by Me or by the world? I allow you that choice, and I invite you to choose life in Me. Do not be estranged, but know instead that you are already with Me. Your spirit knows, and your flesh doubts. Starve the flesh and feed the spirit. Our relationship is unique. Value that. Focus on that, and not on what others have with Me.

I know best what you need to grow, and what you need next as My Bride. Trust the Bridegroom to know more than the Bride. Surrender to Love Himself, and you will not be lost, but found. You will die, but you will also live. Lay aside your garments of control, and put on the garment of trust. I will adorn you, My fairest one, and I will not shame you. Allow Me to reveal to you who I am, and who you are. Step out of the dark and into the light of My presence. In My presence, you will find peace. Be at peace in that you do not have to earn My love—you already have it. Do not hide in shame, as I already know your sins and I still call you to Me. I know that you have betrayed Me, and I give you chances each day to make better choices. You do not need to perfect yourself. That is what I do best.

Stand before Me unashamed, as I see you through eyes of love. I am your Lover, and only I am to be the Judge. Do not judge yourself. Love the one whom I love.

Day 5: Being Named as Beloved

Beloved, let us love one another, for love is of God; and everyone who loves is born of God and knows God. He who does not love does not know God, for God is love.
1 John 4:7-8

Therefore, as the elect of God, holy and beloved, put on tender mercies, kindness, humility, meekness, longsuffering...
Colossians 3:12

Behold what manner of love the Father has bestowed on us, that we should be called children of God! Therefore the world does not know us, because it did not know Him. Beloved, now we are children of God; and it has not yet been revealed what we shall be, but we know that when He is revealed, we shall be like Him, for we shall see Him as He is.
1 John 3:1-2

Beloved,

Hear the sound of that word. Roll the word over and over upon your lips. Do you hear My tenderness toward you? Beloved is your identity. You belong. There is a place for you. Your identity is established. It does not need to be earned, and it cannot be lost.

I am unchangeable and I cannot lie. Beloved, you are accepted and you are known. There is no need to hide. Step into the light of being chosen. Your name is

Beloved. Breathe in the pleasure that you are loved. You are one who is received into the family of God.

You do not need to be like everyone else. I have room in My heart for many individuals. There is freedom in My love. Reach out and grow in My love for you. Step into the possibility of more. My love for you empowers you. You are free to love. Love releases bondages. I am the Bondage Breaker.

Set others free, as you have been set free.

Day 6: Build Me a House of Prayer

Or do you not know that your body is a temple of the Holy Spirit who is in you, whom you have from God, and that you are not your own?
1 Corinthians 6:19 NASB

So then you are no longer strangers and aliens, but you are fellow citizens with the saints, and are of God's household, having been built on the foundation of the apostles and prophets, Christ Jesus Himself being the corner stone, in whom the whole building, being fitted together, is growing into a holy temple in the Lord, in whom you also are being built together into a dwelling of God in the Spirit.
Ephesians 2:19-22 NASB

Dearest One,

Create a space for Me alone. Each day that I have given you has space for Me. Will you enter into it, or let it pass you by? Build a time for Me in which you honor Me. I am here—are you available? I am not unreasonable or demanding. I only ask to be remembered by you daily. As you make time for Me, you will be blessed by growing in My Spirit. Carve out a house of prayer by making time to sit with Me and listen. The foundation of this house is availability. How firm is your foundation?

Pull away from that which entangles you, and step into the space in which My Spirit is waiting. Enter holy ground. I will not disappoint you. The world and the flesh are demanding. Break this hold by strengthening your walk in the Spirit.

Day 7: Calvary

The road to Calvary is paved with many choices.
The choices begin with love and end with love.
Calvary is the place to surrender your way for My way.
I died before the cross. I died to My will.
Calvary was the final surrender,
the ultimate act of love.
Calvary did not just happen—
I chose it, step by step.
Can you follow where I lead?
Can you submit yourself to Me?
Will you choose your own Calvary and die to self,
that I may live in you, and you in Me?
Calvary is not the end, but the beginning.
What looks like death unfolds in life—life in My will.
Can you choose the path that I walk?
Will you walk the path with Me?

Day 8: Choose to be God's Original

Just as a body, though one, has many parts, but all its many parts form one body, so it is with Christ. For we were all baptized by one Spirit so as to form one body—whether Jews or Gentiles, slave or free—and we were all given the one Spirit to drink. Even so the body is not made up of one part but of many.

Now if the foot should say, "Because I am not a hand, I do not belong to the body," it would not for that reason stop being part of the body. And if the ear should say, "Because I am not an eye, I do not belong to the body," it would not for that reason stop being part of the body. If the whole body were an eye, where would the sense of hearing be? If the whole body were an ear, where would the sense of smell be? But in fact God has placed the parts in the body, every one of them, just as he wanted them to be. If they were all one part, where would the body be?

As it is, there are many parts, but one body. The eye cannot say to the hand, "I don't need you!" And the head cannot say to the feet, "I don't need you!" On the contrary, those parts of the body that seem to be weaker are indispensable, and the parts that we think are less honorable we treat with special honor. And the parts that are unpresentable are treated with special modesty, while our presentable parts need no special treatment. But God has put the body together, giving greater honor to the parts that lacked it, so that there should be no division in the body, but that its parts should have equal concern for each other.

1 Corinthians 12:12-25

For you are a holy people to the LORD your God; the LORD your God has chosen you to be a people for Himself, a special treasure above all the peoples on the face of the earth.
Deuteronomy 7:6

My son, do not walk in the way with them,
Keep your foot from their path.
Proverbs 1:15

My Dearest,

I have not overlooked you. I am here, as I always have been. Do not compare yourself to others and find our relationship lacking. I meet each of My Beloveds in unique, personal ways. You perceive these ways as paths of favoritism given to others, but this perception is not the truth. You are much loved by your Creator. Do not enter into that place where you think of yourself as the outcast and all the others as highly favored.

Look at Me and not at the gifts. Look at Me, and I will supply what is needed in the body of Christ. Do you want to be a clone of someone else in the body, or do you want to be who I created you to be? If I wanted you to be like another, you would be so. I create originals. Do not grow impatient with your progress.

Day 9: Choose Better

All things are lawful for me, but all things are not helpful. All things are lawful for me, but I will not be brought under the power of any...Or do you not know that your body is the temple of the Holy Spirit who is in you, whom you have from God, and you are not your own? For you were bought at a price; therefore glorify God in your body and in your spirit, which are God's.
1 Corinthians 6:12, 19-20

But put on the Lord Jesus Christ, and make no provision for the flesh, to fulfill its lusts.
Romans 13:14

Dearest One,

Do not eat over your feelings, and do not eat over the empty spaces in your life. Choose things of life to fill those spaces. Do not stop up your life with overeating, but instead choose wisely from an assortment of life-giving choices. When you are not hungry, forgo the choice to eat, as food will not be what you need; food will only be a familiar want. You can choose again. I call you to the better choice. I am with you, and I give you the strength to choose life, not death.

Day 10: Choose Wisely

To know wisdom and instruction,
To perceive the words of understanding,
To receive the instruction of wisdom,
Justice, judgment, and equity;
To give prudence to the simple,
To the young man knowledge and discretion—
A wise man will hear and increase learning,
And a man of understanding will attain wise counsel...
Turn at my rebuke;
Surely I will pour out my spirit on you;
I will make my words known to you...
Because they hated knowledge
And did not choose the fear of the LORD,
They would have none of my counsel
And despised my every rebuke.
Proverbs 1:2-5, 23, 29-30

Dearest Child,

Choose wisely from the tree of life. Evaluate what is real and what is lasting. Partake of the fruit that bears life, not death. The fruit that leads to death is not always apparent. Discern the fruit carefully. Do not pick everything that is in front of you. Your spirit knows what is best. Your flesh knows what is appealing. They are not the same.

Create life with the time that I give to you. Choice by choice, create something that will bear life. Remember, I permit rest and leisure. Also, remember that what you partake of will stay with you. If you lean against the worldly, the worldly will leave a mark upon you. Be careful where you lean. Be cautious of whose ear you have.

Quiet is needed to penetrate the worldly. Give yourself the gift of quiet in order to release yourself from the pull of this world. Open to that which is eternal, the inner world of the Spirit. Who you spend time with colors who you are. Allow My Holy Spirit to guide you, and you will be refreshed. Choose to be with Me, to listen to Me, and you will not have as much anxiety. Still your busy mind by choosing to rest in My presence. Rest beside the still waters. Renew yourself in Me.

Day 11: Christ Is Your Cover

When my enemies turn back,
They shall fall and perish at Your presence.
Psalm 9:3

He shall cover you with His feathers,
And under His wings you shall take refuge;
His truth shall be your shield and buckler.
Psalm 91:4

Therefore purge out the old leaven, that you may be a new lump, since you truly are unleavened.
For indeed Christ, our Passover,
was sacrificed for us.
1 Corinthians 5:7

The beloved of the LORD
shall dwell in safety by Him,
Who shelters him all the day long;
And he shall dwell between His shoulders.
Deuteronomy 33:12

Dearest,

I cover you as Boaz covered Ruth. I am your Redeemer King, and I will provide richly for you.

I absolve you of your guilt and your shame. You are who I say you are. I am responsible for you, as My blood has covered you and your sins. Get up and sin no more. This is a new day. Rejoice, for I have seen your heart. I have changed your name to Loyal One, Bride of the King. No more will you hide in the shadows of My Kingdom. Come out. I call you into the light of My presence. Walk with Me. You are My beloved one. Listen to what I say, and walk in obedience. I will grow you as you follow in My footsteps.

Day 12: Come Aside With the Lord

"I am the true vine, and My Father is the vinedresser. Every branch in Me that does not bear fruit He takes away; and every branch that bears fruit He prunes, that it may bear more fruit. You are already clean because of the word which I have spoken to you. Abide in Me, and I in you. As the branch cannot bear fruit of itself, unless it abides in the vine, neither can you, unless you abide in Me. I am the vine, you are the branches. He who abides in Me, and I in him, bears much fruit; for without Me you can do nothing."
John 15:1-5

Now it happened as they went that He entered a certain village; and a certain woman named Martha welcomed Him into her house. And she had a sister called Mary, who also sat at Jesus' feet and heard His word. But Martha was distracted with much serving, and she approached Him and said, "Lord, do You not care that my sister has left me to serve alone? Therefore tell her to help me." And Jesus answered and said to her, "Martha, Martha, you are worried and troubled about many things. But one thing is needed, and Mary has chosen that good part, which will not be taken away from her."
Luke 10:38-42

"But you, when you pray, go into your room, and when you have shut your door, pray to your Father who is in the secret place; and your Father who sees in secret will reward you openly."
Matthew 6:6

Dearest One,

In the valley you will find a quietness that will teach you many things. Life flows more simply there, and you do not miss things because of the clutter of busyness. The quiet can seem uneventful, as you do not have the excitement of living on the mountaintops. Do not be anxious to change where I place you. Do not try to bring the mountaintop to the valley. Accept where you are. Live to the fullest where you are now. Be in it. Absorb into your life the lessons I teach you. Ponder My words. Apply them to your life, as they are streams of living water.

You must listen with your heart to hear Me speak to you. Look to your Shepherd, who leads you along your journey. Step back to see where you have been and where I am leading. Appreciate the journey that is uniquely yours. What story am I telling in your life?

Day 13: Come to the Quiet

Surely I have calmed and quieted my soul,
Like a weaned child with his mother;
Like a weaned child is my soul within me.
Psalm 131:2

My soul, wait silently for God alone,
For my expectation is from Him.
Psalm 62:5

I will stand my watch
And set myself on the rampart,
And watch to see what He will say to me,
And what I will answer when I am corrected.
Habakkuk 2:1

My Dear One,

Take time apart and be with Me in the quiet. I will meet you there. This time apart in prayer is sacred time, and I delight when My people honor Me with their love. Do not judge the time as wasted because of the wandering of your mind. It is natural for your mind to wander. The mind will settle down, but it will always be jumping at different ideas, like a fish to bait. Simply be. I ask for no more than obedience in coming aside with Me. The practice of prayer takes time, and true quiet is a gift. Come to give to the Giver of all gifts, and not to receive. If you come to give, you will not be disappointed. If you come expecting, you may leave disappointed.

I am meeting you in a different dimension. Prayer cannot be evaluated as other works can. Come apart in rest, and I will renew you. I will receive your gift of love. Be faithful to the practice of prayer, and more faithful to the One who awaits you in the quiet. In the quiet, you will enter holy ground. I will meet My Beloved at the appointed time. I will be waiting.

Day 14: Come and Rest

Do not let your adorning be external—the braiding of hair and the putting on of gold jewelry, or the clothing you wear—but let your adorning be the hidden person of the heart with the imperishable beauty of a gentle and quiet spirit, which in God's sight is very precious.
1 Peter 3:3-4 ESV

Be still, and know that I am God.
I will be exalted among the nations,
I will be exalted in the earth!
Psalm 46:10 ESV

For thus said the Lord GOD, the Holy One of Israel,
"In returning and rest you shall be saved;
in quietness and in trust shall be your strength."
Isaiah 30:15 ESV

My Beloved,

Come to My heart and meet Me. Behold My love. Enter in and you will find rest. Lean into Me and draw strength from My loving presence.

Love does not demand. My love allows you to be who you truly are. Love does not restrict or expect; love simply loves. There is no fear in love—there is only room for growth. When there are no expectations, and no demands, you are free to become who you were intended to be all along.

Do not doubt that I dwell within you. I have been here all along. I have made you from a desire and I will stay with you until I call you home. Where else would the Creator be, but with His Beloved?

Rest against My heart and be with Me, as I wait for you daily. Will you meet Me and press into My heart? Do you hear Me calling you? Will you come to the silence, or run away from it?

Day 15: Offer Yourself

Listen to me in silence, O coastlands;
let the peoples renew their strength;
let them approach, then let them speak;
let us together draw near for judgment.
Isaiah 41:1 ESV

Immediately Jesus made His disciples get into the boat and go before Him to the other side, while He sent the multitudes away. And when He had sent the multitudes away, He went up on the mountain by Himself to pray. Now when evening came, He was alone there.
Matthew 14:22-23

Be still, and know that I am God;
I will be exalted among the nations,
I will be exalted in the earth!
Psalm 46:10

Dearest Child of Longing,

Here I am in your midst. I am with you as you present yourself to Me in obedience. Keep coming to Me in prayer, and keep this time sacred. Regardless of how you think your prayer "was," I Am. The results are not for you to determine. Simply present the offering of yourself, and I will do with it what I will. It is not your position to critique how your prayer time was ineffective, because of your wandering mind. I do not grade you by your distractions. I look at your heart's intentions, and that is what I see. Give yourself as a gift of love, and I will receive it as that.

Do not place upon Me your attitude toward yourself. That is not how I am. I am much more than you know and experience. Do not give up, for I have called you to this prayer that is so frustrating to you. Do it for Me, and not for you. That is true love. True love is giving to the one you love that which they want from you the most. To pray this way is to stretch yourself beyond your comfort zone, and to place yourself in need of My mercy. All that you need to do is to offer to Me that which I desire from you. You do not need to be perfect; you only need to offer your love to Me the best that you can, and trust the outcome to Me.

Can you place all your frustrations before Me and trust Me to take them? Am I worthy of your trust? Am I not the One who holds you by the hand and leads you? Did I not call you to come and follow Me? Will I not lead you the rest of the way home? I am more than sufficient. Come and see that I am enough.

Day 16: Come, Be With the Lord

*There is therefore now no condemnation
to those who are in Christ Jesus, who do not walk
according to the flesh, but according to the Spirit.
For the law of the Spirit of life in Christ Jesus
has made me free from the law of sin and death.
For what the law could not do in that it was weak
through the flesh, God did by sending His own Son in the
likeness of sinful flesh, on account of sin: He condemned
sin in the flesh, that the righteous requirement of the law
might be fulfilled in us who do not walk according to the
flesh but according to the Spirit.*

*For those who live according to the flesh
set their minds on the things of the flesh, but those who
live according to the Spirit, the things of the Spirit.
For to be carnally minded is death,
but to be spiritually minded is life and peace.
Because the carnal mind is enmity against God; for it is
not subject to the law of God, nor indeed can be.
So then, those who are in the flesh cannot please God.
But you are not in the flesh but in the Spirit, if indeed the
Spirit of God dwells in you. Now if anyone does not have
the Spirit of Christ, he is not His.*

*And if Christ is in you, the body is dead because of sin,
but the Spirit is life because of righteousness. But if the
Spirit of Him who raised Jesus from the dead dwells in
you, He who raised Christ from the dead will also give
life to your mortal bodies through His Spirit who dwells
in you. Therefore, brethren, we are debtors—not to the
flesh, to live according to the flesh. For if you live
according to the flesh you will die; but if by the Spirit
you put to death the deeds of the body, you will live.*

For as many as are led by the Spirit of God, these are sons of God. For you did not receive the spirit of bondage again to fear, but you received the Spirit of adoption by whom we cry out, "Abba, Father." The Spirit Himself bears witness with our spirit that we are children of God, and if children, then heirs—heirs of God and joint heirs with Christ, if indeed we suffer with Him, that we may also be glorified together.
Romans 8:1-17

Dearest,

I do not call you servant; I call you friend. You are a friend of God. Your name is written in the Lamb's Book of Life. You are included. You belong. No longer are you an orphan. Bask in My light. Sit at My feet, dearest one. I will give you manna. Come daily and be fed. You need this manna to grow beyond where you currently are. Will you come to the feast prepared for you? Sit before Me in loving surrender. I am willing—are you? Come to the living waters and drink freely. Choose wisely, and you will drink from the waters of freedom and growth.

Where will you show up? I give you choices. The world can be intoxicating, yet what I offer is eternal. Come to Me. I will teach you. Come to the school of spiritual growth. Your lessons await you. Rest in Me. Be transformed through My life poured out to you. Feed on truth. You get to choose what to feed upon. Come within. I am waiting. Will you wait upon Me.?

I will give you a new heart. Show up for our divine appointments. Come and be transformed. I will wash you of the effects of the world. Your garments will be washed clean. Come to our meeting tent, and rest in My glory. You do not need to see; you only need to believe that you may see the things of the Kingdom. Show up for Me more than you show up for other distractions. Can you make the transition? Do you want to receive more? You get to make that choice. I am your willing Teacher.

Day 17: Come Out of Shame

In you, LORD my God,
I put my trust.
I trust in you;
do not let me be put to shame,
nor let my enemies triumph over me.
No one who hopes in you
will ever be put to shame,
but shame will come on those
who are treacherous without cause.
Psalm 25:1-3 NIV

Guard my life and rescue me;
do not let me be put to shame,
for I take refuge in you.
Psalm 25:20 NIV

In You, O LORD, I put my trust;
Let me never be ashamed;
Deliver me in Your righteousness.
Psalm 31:1 NKJV

Beloved,

Hear Me speak to you a message of value. You are My treasure. I paid the price for you with My very own blood. You were ransomed from darkness and death. I could not forget you. I know who you are. The enemy can only deceive and confuse. I bring clarity and life. My love for you, My Beloved, is beyond measure. I paid the price in full. Your freedom has been won. No longer walk as a prisoner. You are free. You are free. You are free.

Do not put yourself back into captivity by your beliefs. Give Me the lies of the enemy. Trust in Me, as I am trustworthy. Bride of Christ, rise up. Stand before Me in courage. You are My Beloved. No more will you walk in shame. You have dignity, My valuable one. Step out in the truth of your value. You matter in the Kingdom. There is a purpose for you. You are significant. Value has been placed upon you. You are Mine.

Day 18: Comparing Yourself with Others

For we dare not class ourselves or compare ourselves with those who commend themselves. But they, measuring themselves by themselves, and comparing themselves among themselves, are not wise.
2 Corinthians 10:12

Make a careful exploration of who you are and the work you have been given, and then sink yourself into that. Don't be impressed with yourself. Don't compare yourself with others. Each of you must take responsibility for doing the creative best you can with your own life.
Galatians 6:4 MSG

But who are you, a human being, to talk back to God? Shall what is formed say to the one who formed it, "Why did you make me like this?" Does not the potter have the right to make out of the same lump of clay some pottery for special purposes and some for common use?
Romans 9:20-21 NIV

Dearest Listener,

When you listen in hope and faith, I am there. I take no delight in withholding My presence from you, as I am always with you. You may go through periods of silence and dryness, but this does not mean that I have turned My back to you. I work in ways that strengthen you and cause you to grow and seek Me.

Comparison does not work. You cannot look at what I am doing with another and want that repeated in your life, as though you could duplicate that relationship. Why would I have made so many people if there was only one way to relate to Me? No one is at the same place on every level. There may be similarities on many levels, but there are degrees of openness and degrees of brokenness. Being wounded affects what you can give and receive. Do not set yourself up for failure by comparisons. Comparisons are a trap for the one making the comparisons. The trap of comparisons will keep you focused inward on the self, and not on the One with whom you seek to be in relationship.

To trust that I have no favorites is a leap of faith for you. I am your Heavenly Father who created you. I knew from the beginning who you would be, and I still said yes to you. Can you say yes to Me, that I know the plans I have for you, and that those plans are best for you? Stop looking at what others have. I have My plan and My purpose, and My intention is not to punish you, but to make of you what I choose for you. Be content with My plan, even when it conflicts with your plan. You will one day see the whole picture and know why. For now, receive the truth of My love for you. You are also My child, and I never turn My back on you. Your feelings are not reality, but a response to what you perceive as reality. This is why I need to be in charge.

It takes some people longer to change than others because of their history. This is why judging is useless. I am the Potter, and you are the clay. Quit struggling as I mold you. Listen as I tell you of My love for you. When you know that you are loved, you will struggle less and trust more.

I love you as you are. I encourage you to be all that you can become—not because you are not enough, but because I see all of your qualities, and I delight in what I know about you. You will be refined and tested, as well as polished and used. My hands are upon your life in love.

Day 19: Create Time for Him

How lovely is Your tabernacle,
O Lord of hosts!
My soul longs, yes, even faints
For the courts of the Lord;
My heart and my flesh cry out for the living God.
Even the sparrow has found a home,
And the swallow a nest for herself,
Where she may lay her young—
Even Your altars, O Lord of hosts,
My King and my God.
Blessed are those who dwell in Your house;
They will still be praising You. Selah.
...For a day in Your courts is better than a thousand.
I would rather be a doorkeeper in the house of my God
Than dwell in the tents of wickedness.
Psalm 84:1-4, 10

Dearest Listener,

My words to you are My lifeline to you. Hear My words spoken in love. I am with you always. You are never abandoned or forsaken. Rejoice that you are numbered in My Book of Life. Rejoice, and be at rest, My love. You have My ear. Do I have your ear, or are you so busy that you do not realize to whose ear you are turned?

Check in with Me frequently. Do not go on automatic pilot. Focus on Me, and not on all that you need to do. Do you realize that when you give Me all your needs, I will help you to complete those necessary chores?

I will not distract you, but I will empower you to do that which is necessary. Your priority needs to be upon Me, and I will help you with the rest of your day.

Come to Me and be focused. I am your strength. You will find more time in your day when you give Me some of your time. Tithe your time to Me, My Beloved. I will settle you, and I will redirect you. You matter in My Kingdom. It is My pleasure to join you in your life. Come to Me and be renewed.

I will lead you throughout your day. Rest in My presence. Make Me Lord of your day. Each choice matters. Do I matter enough to redirect yourself to Me? You already know the answer to this question. Begin anew this day. Watch for where I am. Be at peace, My love, as I am with you always.

Day 20: Daddy's Tender Love

A father of the fatherless, a defender of widows,
Is God in His holy habitation.
God sets the solitary in families;
He brings out those who are bound into prosperity;
But the rebellious dwell in a dry land.
Psalm 68:5-6

"Therefore do not be like them. For your Father knows the things you have need of before you ask Him....Look at the birds of the air, for they neither sow nor reap nor gather into barns; yet your heavenly Father feeds them. Are you not of more value than they?
Matthew 6:8, 26

"If you then, being evil, know how to give good gifts to your children, how much more will your Father who is in heaven give good things to those who ask Him!"
Matthew 7:11

Dearest Child of the Father,

I am pleased to have rested with you. This surprises you that I could rest with My children. Do I not enjoy the company of the ones I created? Am I not a loving Father? Oh, child, you are worth My time and My attention. This alone is worth pondering. You are valuable to Me, and I desire to be with you. Does this sound too good to be true? The truth is indeed good, and the truth heals. You are not someone to be tolerated; you are someone to treasure. I love the one I created. You are the Father's child, and I will always have time for you.

I have given you others to love you. Some will do this quite well, and others will do it imperfectly. People are flawed in different ways. Look for the beauty in the flaws. Focusing on the beauty is sometimes more difficult to do when those you love hurt you because of their own pain and struggles. Their intent is not to be cruel, but their pain leaks out and colors intentions. Come back to Daddy, and tell Me how you feel. I will not disappoint you. Be still and know that I am God.

Day 21: Delight Yourself in the Lord

Like an apple tree among the trees of the woods,
So is my beloved among the sons.
I sat down in his shade with great delight,
And his fruit was sweet to my taste.
Song of Solomon 2:3

Though you have not seen him, you love him; and even though you do not see him now, you believe in him and are filled with an inexpressible and glorious joy.
1 Peter 1:8

Delight yourself also in the Lord,
And He shall give you the desires of your heart.
Psalm 37:4

Dearest,

Delight yourself in Me, My delightful one. Do you see My heart for you? Does My love warm your heart toward Me? Rest in the knowledge that you are secure in My love. Have spiritual confidence in your identity in Me.

I am delighted to be loved by you, My dearest. Think lovingly of Me, as I think lovingly of you. Rest in the bliss of My love. Allow My love to settle into you. Soak in My loving presence. This will change the atmosphere around you.

Day 22: Desire the Lord

One thing I have desired of the Lord,
That will I seek:
That I may dwell in the house of the Lord
All the days of my life,
To behold the beauty of the Lord,
And to inquire in His temple....
When You said, "Seek My face,"
My heart said to You, "Your face, Lord, I will seek."
Psalm 27:4,8

O God, You are my God;
Early will I seek You;
My soul thirsts for You;
My flesh longs for You
In a dry and thirsty land
Where there is no water.
So I have looked for You in the sanctuary,
To see Your power and Your glory.
Because Your lovingkindness is better than life,
My lips shall praise You.
Thus I will bless You while I live;
I will lift up my hands in Your name.

My soul shall be satisfied as with marrow and fatness,
And my mouth shall praise You with joyful lips.
When I remember You on my bed,
I meditate on You in the night watches.
Because You have been my help,
Therefore in the shadow of Your wings I will rejoice.
My soul follows close behind You;
Your right hand upholds me.
Psalm 63:1-8

My Dearest,

I see the beauty of your heart that longs for more of Me. I desire you to experience more of My presence. I want My Bride to fully experience My presence that is always with you. I will draw you to Me with gentle cords of loving tenderness. My embrace will create in you a desire for more of Me.

Are you hungry, My dear one? I alone can quench your hunger. Taste and see that the Lord is good. I delight in your hunger and thirst. Come and drink freely—you will not be denied. Do not hold yourself back. Come boldly to the throne. I am present, and I am yours.

Day 23: Do Not Be a Target

...but, speaking the truth in love, may grow up in all things into Him who is the head—Christ.
Ephesians 4:15

Therefore, since we have such hope, we use great boldness of speech.
2 Corinthians 3:12

"Be angry, and do not sin": do not let the sun go down on your wrath, nor give place to the devil.
Ephesians 4:26-27

Dearest One Who Is Hurting,

You have not valued yourself, and you look to others for your value. Sometimes you are fed by the overflow of people's loving reception of you. Other times there is a drought of response to you, and you pick up the arrows of wounded people's humanity shot in your direction. Step away from being a target. Give Me the arrows. Do not receive the arrows, as they are from the enemy, who uses wounded people to hurt you. Tell yourself to stop receiving the arrows, and learn to deflect them. You do not need to absorb what is said. You can speak up with kindness and authority.

Day 24: Draw Closer to the Lord

Draw near to God and He will draw near to you.
Cleanse your hands, you sinners; and purify your hearts, you double-minded.
James 4:8

And the Lord, He is the one who goes before you.
He will be with you, He will not leave you
nor forsake you; do not fear nor be dismayed."
Deuteronomy 31:8

"Have I not commanded you?
Be strong and of good courage;
do not be afraid, nor be dismayed,
for the Lord your God
is with you wherever you go."
Joshua 1:9

Dearest Beloved,

I am with you always. Fear not—you are never alone. I will never forsake you. My back will never be to you. Come into My presence. I say "come" because it is possible to enter into My presence. Your previous experiences do not dictate your future experiences. Faith is active. Our relationship is alive. Our relationship is not rote, like going through ritualistic movements. I am alive in you. Come alive in the Spirit. Awaken, spirit man. Faith is not dead motions. I am with you, and you are with Me. Your feelings are not an indication of what is happening on a spiritual level.

Speak to Me more, as I am always with you. I am not a spiritual chore to get done before the day is over. I am alive, and our relationship needs to be alive. Speak to Me. Ask Me questions. Do not put Me in one part of the day—allow Me to be in all of your day. Be in union with Me. Pray in the Spirit. When you do this, you will grow spiritually. Practice speaking to Me more, and you will experience Me more. Make time and take time.

Day 25: Drop Seeds of Hope

Then He said to His disciples, "The harvest truly is plentiful, but the laborers are few. Therefore pray the Lord of the harvest to send out laborers into His harvest."
Matthew 9:37-38

How then shall they call on Him in whom they have not believed? And how shall they believe in Him of whom they have not heard? And how shall they hear without a preacher?
Romans 10:14

How beautiful upon the mountains
Are the feet of him who brings good news,
Who proclaims peace,
Who brings glad tidings of good things,
Who proclaims salvation,
Who says to Zion,
"Your God reigns!"
Isaiah 52:7

Dearest,

Drop seeds of hope and love as you walk along your path of life. Others will hunger for crumbs. They will look for signs that I live. Give them a reason to believe. Reflect Me to others. Feed them My presence.

Day 26: During the Storms of Life

Fear not, for I am with you;
Be not dismayed, for I am your God.
I will strengthen you, Yes, I will help you,
I will uphold you with My righteous right hand.
Isaiah 41:10

Many are the afflictions of the righteous,
But the Lord delivers him out of them all.
Psalm 34:19

Be merciful to me, O God, be merciful to me!
For my soul trusts in You;
And in the shadow of Your wings
I will make my refuge,
Until these calamities have passed by.
Psalm 57:1

Come to Me, all you who labor and are heavy laden, and I will give you rest. Take My yoke upon you and learn from Me, for I am gentle and lowly in heart, and you will find rest for your souls. For My yoke is easy and My burden is light.
Matthew 11:28-30

Dearest Child,

Believe in Me and who I am in your life. I am able to still the waves of your life in but a moment of time. I am walking beside you on your journey during these turbulent times. I have not left you alone, but I am supporting you through a sea of difficulties.

You are not the problem. The problem is the pain. Pain writes a script in people's lives, and it is acted out through their lives. People in pain can say that you are to blame for their problems, but their pain over unresolved areas of their life is what is speaking to you and at you. You may have done something small or even large, but it is their pain that will develop it further into something of a bigger picture. Pain is a distorted lens through which to view life. Pain contaminates relationships.

It is possible to step back and see the picture from another perspective. Lean away from the pain that is being directed at you. You are not to get in the middle of it, but turn to Me to deflect it from you. I will keep you during this time, as a raincoat keeps you dry when it is raining. Put on My presence through relationship with Me. Nestle into Me, and I will keep you safe and dry during the storms of life. Storms cannot be avoided, but they can be prepared for. Know where your safe shelter is and seek it. I am your high tower and in Me you will find safety.

I am your Father, and I will carry you when you are too weary to walk the rest of the way. I will allow you to walk when I know that you can walk. I will empower you, but I will not enable you. You are safe in My arms. Trust Me, even when I say, "Walk."

Day 27: Encouragement in Love

I love those who love me,
And those who seek me diligently will find me.
Proverbs 8:17

Then you will call upon Me and go and pray to Me, and I will listen to you. And you will seek Me and find Me, when you search for Me with all your heart. I will be found by you, says the Lord, and I will bring you back from your captivity; I will gather you from all the nations and from all the places where I have driven you, says the Lord, and I will bring you to the place from which I cause you to be carried away captive.
Jeremiah 29:12-14

Seek the Lord and His strength;
Seek His face evermore!
1 Chronicles 16:11

Dearest One,

You are dear to Me, My Beloved. I await our times of meeting in the secret place. Keep seeking Me and you will find Me. I wait to be found by you.

You sometimes doubt My love for you, as though you are unlovable. Do you not know that I see you with eyes of love? I know My Beloved and My Beloved is Mine. I search for you, and you in turn search for Me. You are building stones of faithfulness in your journey to Me.

Keep taking time with Me and I will give you time with Me.

I behold your heart and I mark it as mine. May I have your heart, Beloved? I give you My heart, as it is yours for the asking. I am a generous God and I lavish My love upon you. Receive what is being offered.

My heart is a refuge—seek refuge. My heart is a well—drink deeply. The resources of Heaven are at your disposal. Ask freely. I am extravagant.

Day 28: You Are Heard

You know my sitting down and my rising up;
You understand my thought afar off....
For there is not a word on my tongue,
But behold, O Lord, You know it altogether.
Psalm 139:2, 4

It shall come to pass
That before they call,
I will answer;
And while they are still speaking,
I will hear.
Isaiah 65:24

The Lord has appeared of old to me, saying:
"Yes, I have loved you with an everlasting love;
Therefore with lovingkindness I have drawn you."
Jeremiah 31:3

Call to Me, and I will answer you,
and show you great and mighty things,
which you do not know.
Jeremiah 33:3

Dearest,

Is My arm too short to bless you? Am I so far away that I should lose sight of you? Can I not hear the longings of your heart? Am I not He who formed your heart and fashioned you out of dust? I see. I hear. I know. I am.

My dearest, I will not forsake you. I care for you as I care for My Son, Jesus. You can contemplate that for all of eternity. I love you, and I am working in your life. Watch and see what I will do.

Day 29: Encouragement in Prayer

The Lord is good to those who wait for Him,
To the soul who seeks Him.
Lamentations 3:25

The Lord God is my strength;
He will make my feet like deer's feet,
And He will make me walk on my high hills.
Habakkuk 3:19

Why are you cast down, O my soul?
And why are you disquieted within me?
Hope in God, for I shall yet praise Him
For the help of His countenance.
O my God, my soul is cast down within me;
Therefore I will remember You
from the land of the Jordan,
And from the heights of Hermon,
From the Hill Mizar.
Psalm 42:5-6

Dearest One,

I say that you are one who waits impatiently, because after all this time you forget who you are, and who I am. You cannot lose Me. I am the One who leads you. Rest in Me, even if you feel nothing. I am the Shepherd. If the pastures seem dry, water them with your love and faithfulness. Do what you can do, and know that I have given you My Holy Spirit to teach you what you need to know. Come back to what you know, not to what you feel. Do not make an idol of your feelings, and do not make experiences or lack of experiences a stumbling block.

Do not focus on what is wrong in prayer; focus on Me. I already know how dry your prayer life is. You do not need to convince Me. Convince yourself that praying is prayer, and that resting in My presence is exactly that. Do not hate your prayer life because it does not nurture your flesh. Am I not the object of your prayer? Seek Me. I will be found by those who diligently seek Me. Do not be discouraged, My little one who wants so much. Put on your spiritual blinders and follow Me.

Prayer is not about you. It is all about Me. Start again in childlike faith. I am patient and I am waiting for you. I know where you are and what you are doing. I am not asleep and I see you. Keep looking and you will see. Keep listening and you will hear. Keep loving and you will feel loved. Get back up and begin again.

Day 30: He Longs for You

As the deer pants for the water brooks,
So pants my soul for You, O God.
My soul thirsts for God, for the living God.
When shall I come and appear before God?
Psalm 42:1-2

Be strong and of good courage,
do not fear nor be afraid of them;
for the Lord your God,
He is the One who goes with you.
He will not leave you nor forsake you.
Deuteronomy 31:6

Therefore we do not lose heart.
Even though our outward man is perishing,
yet the inward man is being renewed day by day.
For our light affliction, which is but for a moment, is working for us a far more exceeding and eternal weight of glory, while we do not look at the things which are seen, but at the things which are not seen.
For the things which are seen are temporary,
but the things which are not seen are eternal.
2 Corinthians 4:16-18

Dearest Beloved,

My love for you is everlasting. I will always speak to you, My beloved one. You are in My heart, as I am in yours. Do not grow weary or discouraged. Fan the flame of our love. I call you to come closer to Me in a dance of intimacy. Thirst for Me, My dear one. Hunger for My presence.

As a hind longs for the water brooks, so does My heart long for yours. This is reciprocal, is it not? Would not the Bridegroom so long for His Bride? My soul longs for you. Do not worry about not having enough love for Me. I see into your heart, and it pleases Me. I will ignite the passion in your heart. You are neither cold nor lukewarm. I will set your heart ablaze with love. You have remained faithful to Me.

I will not lead you into a maze that is confusing. I want to be found. Cross the threshold of unbelief, and step into a new direction. The path of love is for you, too. I will draw you to Me with cords of love. Believe that you can have what you desire—a vibrant relationship with your Beloved. I will be found by you. In fact, I am already here. Come closer, and see in the Spirit that I am always with you. Do not compare your walk with another. I am a personal God who meets you in a way that is unique for you. You are not too difficult or complicated for Me. I am able to reach into your heart.

Day 31: Every Day is a Gift from God

If you then, being evil, know how to give good gifts to your children, how much more will your Father who is in heaven give good things to those who ask Him!
Matthew 7:11

This is the day the Lord has made;
We will rejoice and be glad in it.
Psalm 118:24

When you walk, your steps will not be hindered,
And when you run, you will not stumble.
Proverbs 4:12

My Child,

Today I gave you life. Choose life. Choose to break the bread I have placed before you. Do not see scraps. Do not see leftovers. See life. I give it to you in abundance. See the life before you from My eyes. Partake of what I choose for you, knowing that I have the best in store for you. What I have allowed to come to you will be for My glory. Do not waste even the pain and the suffering. You are not alone in your pain. No, you are united with My body, which also suffers. Unite with them, and not with the pain. Unite with them in love and compassion.

Remember others who are forgotten in their pain. Reach out to others who need prayer and who feel alone. If one suffers, all suffer. Be aware of others. Pray for others and your prayer will break through to the heavens. Do not let your sufferings make you a prisoner. Look beyond yourself and pray for others. I am here waiting to hear your prayers.

Day 32: Father's Nurturing Love

But now, thus says the LORD,
who created you, O Jacob,
And He who formed you, O Israel:
"Fear not, for I have redeemed you;
I have called you by your name; You are Mine.
Isaiah 43:1

Even so it is not the will of your Father who is in heaven
that one of these little ones should perish.
Matthew 18:14

Most assuredly, I say to you, whatever you ask the
Father in My name He will give you.
John 16:23

Dearest One,

Daddy likes the time that we spend in quiet. You are not lost to Me, My child. Your wounding does not keep Me at a distance from you. Hear Me whisper, "Here I am. I am your Beloved and you are Mine."

I have seen your heart. Let Me heal you in quiet times spent with Me. Come and nestle with your Father. I am not an absentee Father. I am a loving Father who knows the names of all His children. Do you think that I am unaware of your heart's desires and needs? Fear not—I am ever attentive to you, My dear one. I do not place you in a holding place because of your flaws and the unfinished business of your heart. Your heart is My business. I am not offended by the challenges you experience in coming into My presence. You do not always recognize My presence, but this does not negate My continual presence with you. Keep believing and having hope, as I am faithful to you. I want to show you more, and you shall see more. Keep coming closer. Your efforts matter. I see you. I am not excluding you from My Kingdom work. Do not give up, and do not become discouraged. You are not too challenging for Me. The Teacher will lead you to Me. Do what you can, and I will do what I can. Nothing is impossible for Me. I have all the resources that you need. I open doors and I close doors. You are not a mystery to Me.

Make every effort to draw closer to Me. The time you spend in My presence is valuable. Make time to be a student. Impart what you learn into the lives of those around you. Do not think that you are forgotten or too old to use in My Kingdom. Be aware of the moments I give to you. See what you can do to bring life into the world around you. Ask Me to show you how to do this, and I will do so. As you lay down things for Me, I will open doors for you. Exchange the worldly for the godly. Be in the world, but do not let the world be your home. I am your home and your identity. Be filled and pour out, that My seed may be scattered in the world.

Day 33: Financial Generosity

For where your treasure is, there your heart will be also. No one can serve two masters; for either he will hate the one and love the other, or else he will be loyal to the one and despise the other. You cannot serve God and mammon.
Matthew 6:21, 24

Moreover, brethren, we make known to you the grace of God bestowed on the churches of Macedonia: that in a great trial of affliction the abundance of their joy and their deep poverty abounded in the riches of their liberality. For I bear witness that according to their ability, yes, and beyond their ability, they were freely willing, imploring us with much urgency that we would receive the gift and the fellowship of the ministering to the saints....For you know the grace of our Lord Jesus Christ, that though He was rich, yet for your sakes He became poor, that you through His poverty might become rich.
2 Corinthians 8:1-4, 9

The earth is the Lord's, and all its fullness,
The world and those who dwell therein.
Psalm 24:1

Now Jesus sat opposite the treasury and saw how the people put money into the treasury. And many who were rich put in much. Then one poor widow came and threw in two mites, which make a quadrans. So He called His disciples to Himself and said to them, "Assuredly, I say to you that this poor widow has put in more than all those who have given to the treasury; for they all put in out of their abundance, but she out of her poverty put in all that she had, her whole livelihood."
Mark 12:41-44

Beloved,

I am taking you to a place of generosity. Can you give to one who will not embrace you or your beliefs? How generous is your heart toward one who does not value what you value? You do not like to be used by man. Man has used Me for years and years. They wanted what I could give them, but they did not want Me.

You have the resources of your heavenly Father. Lean into My presence and do not lean into your finances. Where is your strength and comfort? You will not find them in your finances. I am the One to turn to. Stand for Me and stand next to Me.

Day 34: Find Rest in the Lord

Turn at my rebuke;
Surely I will pour out my spirit on you;
I will make my words known to you.
Proverbs 1:23

Be still, and know that I am God;
I will be exalted among the nations,
I will be exalted in the earth!
Psalm 46:10

For thus says the Lord God, the Holy One of Israel:
"In returning and rest you shall be saved;
In quietness and confidence shall be your strength."
Isaiah 30:15

Come to Me, all you who labor and are heavy laden, and I will give you rest. Take My yoke upon you and learn from Me, for I am gentle and lowly in heart, and you will find rest for your souls. For My yoke is easy and My burden is light.
Matthew 11:28-30

Dearest Child,

Listen, as I speak to you in the depths of your soul. The silence conducts My message to you. Honor time apart spent in silent waiting. Keep watch with Me awhile. In faith, come to Me, and I will be with you. Do not listen to the voice of doubt. Banish doubt. Why would a Creator not speak to His creation? Why would He create and be silent, as if in hiding from the ones He holds beloved?

You are My Beloved, as you love Me and keep coming back in faith, hope, and love. If someone no longer answered your call, you would not continue calling for long. If someone stopped speaking to you, you would cease attempting to engage the person in conversation. Yet, you keep coming to Me, because I am real and present. I do speak to you deep within.

I am not in hiding from you, but I await your coming to Me in anticipation. I delight in you, My child. You are My created, chosen one. I do not put up with you out of a benevolent nature. I am Love, and I create out of love, and I create love. You are loved, and you come from love, and you will return to Love. This is truth to cling to.

Come home to Me regularly. Rest in your true nature. Rest in the presence of One who knows best. Rest in the presence of loving acceptance. Be restored. Renew yourself in truth. Allow what was to fall away, and what is to come forth. I Am. I am within you, and I will be forevermore.

Day 35: Freedom to Be Yourself

The Lord is my light and my salvation;
Whom shall I fear?
The Lord is the strength of my life;
Of whom shall I be afraid?
When the wicked came against me
To eat up my flesh,
My enemies and foes,
They stumbled and fell.
Though an army may encamp against me,
My heart shall not fear;
Though war should rise against me,
In this I will be confident.
One thing I have desired of the Lord,
That will I seek:
That I may dwell in the house of the Lord
All the days of my life,
To behold the beauty of the Lord,
And to inquire in His temple.
Psalm 27:1-4

For we are His workmanship, created in Christ Jesus for good works, which God prepared beforehand that we should walk in them.
Ephesians 2:10

And do not be conformed to this world, but be transformed by the renewing of your mind, that you may prove what is that good and acceptable and perfect will of God.
Romans 12:2

Dearest One,

Come to life. Step forth in truth and courage. Do not apologize for the life you have. You have a definite place and purpose upon this earth that an imitation will not fulfill. Dare to be your unique self. Listen to who I say you are. Others' impressions are not always accurate. They may see only dimly, or through eyes of pain, and not of love. Only the Creator can fully say who His creation is. Listen, and I will reveal the gift of life that you are. Be born this day in truth and freedom.

Dare to speak one truth at a time. With each venture of who you are and how you feel, believe that you will blossom and become the fullness of who you truly are. Burst forth into your true self. It is up to others to do the same. When you alter your truth and your life to please another, you deny them the same chance to become who they really are.

Through struggle and pain, we emerge into life. Life begins with this struggle, and life ends with this struggle. Do not deny others their struggle to become their true selves by holding back your life process. You do no favors to others by being other than authentic. Your authenticity may call them forth because of the struggle they experience with who you really are. Let them struggle and bring forth their own life.

Do not hold back the life that is stirring in you. New life not permitted to exist becomes depression or illness. You have a right to your opinions, and you have a right to be yourself. You have a birthright in Me. Your being alive is proof enough. Do not give away your birthright. Dare to stand in your uniqueness. You can learn and reassess, but never until you take a chance of bringing to life who you really are.

This is a day of freedom. Give yourself a gift that has been given to you. Be My child. Be My life to the world. Be My message, not another's message. Be Mine.

Day 36: Give the Lord Your Time

But seek first the kingdom of God and His righteousness, and all these things shall be added to you.
Matthew 6:33

And Jesus answered and spoke to them again by parables and said: "The kingdom of heaven is like a certain king who arranged a marriage for his son, and sent out his servants to call those who were invited to the wedding; and they were not willing to come. Again, he sent out other servants, saying, "Tell those who are invited, 'See, I have prepared my dinner; my oxen and fatted cattle are killed, and all things are ready. Come to the wedding.'" But they made light of it and went their ways, one to his own farm, another to his business. And the rest seized his servants, treated them spitefully, and killed them. But when the king heard about it, he was furious. And he sent out his armies, destroyed those murderers, and burned up their city. Then he said to his servants, "The wedding is ready, but those who were invited were not worthy. Therefore go into the highways, and as many as you find, invite to the wedding." So those servants went out into the highways and gathered together all whom they found, both bad and good. And the wedding hall was filled with guests. But when the king came in to see the guests, he saw a man there who did not have on a wedding garment. So he said to him, "Friend, how did you come in here without a wedding garment?" And he was speechless. Then the king said to the servants, "Bind him hand and foot, take him away, and cast him into outer darkness; there will be weeping and gnashing of teeth."
For many are called, but few are chosen.
Matthew 22:1-14

And we desire that each one of you show the same diligence to the full assurance of hope until the end, that you do not become sluggish, but imitate those who through faith and patience inherit the promises.
Hebrews 6:11-12

Dearest One,

It is good to take time once more to listen for My still, small voice. I love when you listen to Me. I am more than willing to speak, if you will but take the time to listen to Me.

The stillness is a place where we can meet face to face in the Spirit. Offer to Me the gift of your time. I am here waiting for you. Are you here waiting for Me?

Come back to Me, my love. Do not let busyness keep us apart. My love for you is everlasting. Will you fit Me into your day?

Day 37: Turn to the Lord

...redeeming the time, because the days are evil.
Ephesians 5:16

According to the grace of God
which was given to me, as a wise master builder
I have laid the foundation, and another builds on it. But
let each one take heed how he builds on it.
1 Corinthians 3:10

Abide in Me, and I in you.
As the branch cannot bear fruit of itself,
unless it abides in the vine,
neither can you, unless you abide in Me.
John 15:4

I beseech you therefore, brethren,
by the mercies of God, that you present your bodies a
living sacrifice, holy, acceptable to God,
which is your reasonable service.
Romans 12:1

Dear Bride of Mine,

I receive your efforts to come closer to Me. I am pleased when you give Me your time. Be generous, My love. I love when you lavish Me with your gifts of time.

Receive My Spirit poured out upon you. When you prime the pump of prayer, My Holy Spirit is released in you. Rest in the presence of My love for you. Anoint yourself with My Word. My Word is living and it will live in you as you partake of it. Live in the strength of My Word.

Refresh yourself in Me. If you are tired, pray more, not less. When you are weary, turn to Me. I will give you rivers of living waters to revive you.

Day 38: God Calls You A Gift

Every good gift and every perfect gift is from above, and comes down from the Father of lights, with whom there is no variation or shadow of turning.
James 1:17

For You formed my inward parts;
You covered me in my mother's womb.
I will praise You,
for I am fearfully and wonderfully made;
Marvelous are Your works,
And that my soul knows very well.
My frame was not hidden from You,
When I was made in secret,
And skillfully wrought
in the lowest parts of the earth.
Your eyes saw my substance, being yet unformed.
And in Your book they all were written,
The days fashioned for me,
When as yet there were none of them.
Psalm 139:13-16

For this reason I remind you to kindle afresh the gift of God which is in you through the laying on of my hands.
2 Timothy 1:6 NAS

Dearest One,

My will for you, My child, is that you accept yourself as whole and beautiful. See yourself as a gift. You are not the empty box waiting for the gift to be put inside. You are not the wrapping paper that adorns the gift box. You are also not the bow that tops off the neatly wrapped gift. You are more—much more than the container, the covering, and the adornment. You are the gift inside.

You are My life, My presence in the world. I breathe within your body. I speak within you. I wait to be given away within you, and I wait to be given to in you. I am in you and you are in Me. You are good and you are a gift. You are a life that will never be repeated again. You are My words, which will only be spoken through you. You are a treasure of life and love, being lived but once in your lifetime. You are that unique expression of Me, given to yourself, and presented to the world.

Do not snuff out that beauty within you. Do not put out your light by devaluing your worth. Take into you the life that I have given to you. Breathe in. Breathe out. Know that My presence is there. You do not need to see. You just need to believe. By your deeds, you will say you believe that you are a gift of God—someone to love and to be loved, someone who values and who has value. You are someone who counts, and will not be discounted, even by yourself. You are My gift, My treasure, purchased at a price that deserves no discount, but praise and joy. Do not take the life I have given to you lightly.

Your life is your responsibility. You are the steward of My gift to you and to the world. Do not be your worst enemy. Love that which was given to you. Love how and who I have chosen to come into the world again. Love the circumstances, the surroundings that are uniquely yours. Do not keep your eyes upon how I have come in others' lives and wonder if I came more grandly or profoundly in their lives.

Each person is a message, a statement that will come but once. Each is a note to the music of life. You are a song to be sung, an instrument to play and to be played in a symphony of life. Without each yes, each lived life, the world misses out on that note, that song, that instrument that is needed for completion of My song to mankind.

I am here among you and within you. Look no further, but look within. Reclaim the treasure of My presence within. Look within and you will find all that you long for. All that you seek is within. I will not leave you an orphan. I will not abandon you. Come within and be with Me.

Day 39: God Is Your Father

In that hour Jesus rejoiced in the Spirit and said, "I thank You, Father, Lord of heaven and earth, that You have hidden these things from the wise and prudent and revealed them to babes. Even so, Father, for so it seemed good in Your sight. All things have been delivered to Me by My Father, and no one knows who the Son is except the Father, and who the Father is except the Son, and the one to whom the Son wills to reveal Him."
Luke 10:21-22

Jesus said to him, "Have I been with you so long, and yet you have not known Me, Philip? He who has seen Me has seen the Father; so how can you say, 'Show us the Father'? Do you not believe that I am in the Father, and the Father in Me? The words that I speak to you I do not speak on My own authority; but the Father who dwells in Me does the works. Believe Me that I am in the Father and the Father in Me, or else believe Me for the sake of the works themselves."
John 14:9-11

Behold what manner of love
the Father has bestowed on us,
that we should be called children of God!
Therefore the world does not know us,
because it did not know Him.
1 John 3:1

Dear Listener,

I listen to you. You are seen and heard, My love. I see you, and I see your heart. I have fashioned you, My dearest. How could I forget you? I am not a "deadbeat dad." Wait upon Me, as I am merciful and full of grace toward you. I give you light, and I delight to bless you. As you bless others, I will pour out Heaven's blessings upon you. I speak to you. Continue to press in to hear My voice.

Press into My loving presence. I will be there. When you show up, so will I. I have been here all along, My dear one. I love you, My Beloved, My treasure. You have been lost, but now you are found. Hide and abide in Me. I am your strength. I remember you.

Day 40: God's Desires for You

Commit your way to the Lord;
trust in him and he will do this...
Psalm 37:5 NIV

"For I know the plans I have for you,"
declares the LORD,
"plans to prosper you and not to harm you,
plans to give you hope and a future."
Jeremiah 29:11 NIV

But indeed for this purpose I have raised you up,
that I may show My power in you, and that My name
may be declared in all the earth.
Exodus 9:16

Dearest,

I listen in you and to you. I listen to hear your heart surrender to My will. Will you believe in my goodness to you when you are experiencing pain and loss? Can you see beyond what you desire to the bigger picture of My desire for you? My desire for you is great. Do not allow the pain in your life to break your faith in My plans for you.

Be a light in dark places to those who hurt. Carry that gift from Me. Welcome others with My joy at seeing them. They are not numbers passing by, but individuals of value who count. Will you count yourself as one who counts and deserves to be counted, and not discounted? Will you value who I value, or will you devalue yourself, disbelieving that I could value you?

Day 41: God's Word Is Life

So now, brethren, I commend you to God
and to the word of His grace, which is able to build you up and give you an inheritance among all those who are sanctified.
Acts 20:32

It is the Spirit who gives life;
the flesh profits nothing.
The words that I speak to you are spirit,
and they are life.
John 6:63

All Scripture is given by inspiration of God,
and is profitable for doctrine,
for reproof, for correction,
for instruction in righteousness,
that the man of God may be complete,
thoroughly equipped for every good work.
2 Timothy 3:16-17

My Child,

Read My Word and let it identify you as a member of the family of God. My Book is not just about strangers; it is about you, as well as for you. Connect to it as history, past and present. I will speak to you in new ways through My Word. My Word is not meant to confuse you or to discourage you, but to encourage you and to give you life.

My Word will be understood in the Spirit. Trust My Spirit to instruct you. Receive My enlightenment, which I give to you. Run to My Word, not from it. I am here with you, and I am in My Word. Look for Me and you will find Me. I intend to be found by those I love—those I call My own.

Day 42: God's Word to You

My sheep hear My voice,
and I know them,
and they follow Me.
And I give them eternal life,
and they shall never perish;
neither shall anyone snatch them out of My hand.
John 10:27-28

So shall My word be
that goes forth from My mouth;
It shall not return to Me void,
But it shall accomplish what I please,
And it shall prosper in the thing for which I sent it.
Isaiah 55:11

As His divine power has given to us all things
that pertain to life and godliness,
through the knowledge of Him
who called us by glory and virtue.
2 Peter 1:3

Dearest Beloved One,

I am with you, even when I am silent. I speak, and My Word goes out like ripples in a lake. My Word is still rippling in this world. My Word is still active in your life. Go to the last Word from Me. My Word is working in you and for you, if you embrace it in agreement. I am the Living Word. I speak, and life occurs. I spoke creation into being.

Do not concern yourself about how long it may have been since I last spoke to you. I spoke, and I am still speaking. Step out into the living waters of My words to you. Live in them and draw life from them. Be refreshed and be renewed. It is not too late to revisit old words to you. You honor Me when you honor what I have said and am saying. Allow My words to wash over you. You are alive, and My Word is alive in you. Be refreshed this day in truth. Your identity is in Me.

Do not go to other words that do not bring life, and that do not line up with what I say. Do not revisit them as if to find new revelation in them. These words are not words of life. Lay them down and surrender to My words, which transform you. My words are life to your body and to your spirit. Choose life this day. My words will not return to Me void. Be strengthened in your inner man.

Day 43: God's Words to You Are Healing

My son, give attention to my words;
Incline your ear to my sayings.
Do not let them depart from your eyes;
Keep them in the midst of your heart;
For they are life to those who find them,
And health to all their flesh.
Keep your heart with all diligence,
For out of it spring the issues of life.
Proverbs 4:20-23

...casting all your care upon Him,
for He cares for you.
1 Peter 5:7

He heals the brokenhearted
And binds up their wounds.
Psalm 147:3

Dear One,

Behold the truth and meditate upon it. Hold My words in your mind and in your heart. Find comfort and joy in them. Count on them, and allow them to be your foundation. Rest in My words, and renew yourself in them. My words will wash away the effect of other words spoken in judgment, cruelty, and unkindness.

Come to the well and drink freely. I call you to come and sit at the feet of Him who knows all. My word to you is to come and follow Me. See where I live. Believe that I dwell within you. Run to Me, and not from Me. Run into the shelter of My welcoming arms. Dare to believe the truth. Trust Me and not the deceiver, who comes but to rob, steal, and destroy. Do not be loyal to his lies. Align yourself with Me, and you will stand. Give your ear to the prince of darkness, and you will falter. Only truth prevails. Draw near to the truth, and allow it to satisfy your deepest longing to belong and to be loved. Do not be fed by the father of lies. Drink from the living stream of life eternal.

You have chosen the better portion, and you have broken bread with truth. This is where your loyalty lies. Make your home in Me, as I will make My home in you.

Do not be afraid to lean against Me. I am your strong tower, and I will not sway. I am your hiding place, and I will not betray you. I have given everything to you, and I have given everything for you. After all this, why would I turn from the one who seeks Me? I await My people's love. I desire their desire of their Savior.

I am a personal God, and not a distant one. This good news remains a secret to many people. You have heard the truth, and you know Me, even though you still harbor doubts. If you accept the truths that I tell you, you will need to let go of the lies you have believed that are still imbedded in your foundation. Now, I call you to start again. This is not a punishment, but progress. Take it one day at a time. Turn to Me with questions. I am your Teacher. I give you My Spirit to guide you.

Day 44: Good Friday

It is finished.
There is nothing more to do.
I have completed My Father's business.
I have crossed the line into eternity.
Now it is your turn.
You are called to die to your will,
and to embrace your Father's will.
Will you look beyond your pain,
to see those whom I love?
Will you pour out your life,
that others may know My Father?
Will you say yes, as I did?
Will you follow the blood of the Lamb
that leads to the cross, to the grave,
and beyond to eternity?

Day 45: Growing Spiritually

But grow in the grace and knowledge
of our Lord and Savior Jesus Christ.
To Him be the glory both now and forever. Amen.
2 Peter 3:18

His divine power has given to us all things that pertain to life and godliness, through the knowledge of Him who called us by glory and virtue, by which have been given to us exceedingly great and precious promises, that through these you may be partakers of the divine nature.
2 Peter 1:3

As you have therefore received
Christ Jesus the Lord,
so walk in Him, rooted and built up in Him
and established in the faith,
as you have been taught,
abounding in it with thanksgiving.
Colossians 2:6-7

Dearest Beloved,

My hand is upon your life. Can you look to see My handprints I have left for you? I want you to believe in My presence that is always with you. Believe and you shall see Me. I am in plain sight, if you have eyes of faith to see Me. Your faith grows when you can remember where I have been in your life. Trust in where I will be next in your life. This is not a risk or a gamble.

I am reliable and true. Test Me and see that I am dependable. Open your eyes and be renewed in My reliability. I will neither leave you nor forsake you. I am invested in your life. This is a new journey that you are taking. Step out and see Me around you. Grow your faith muscle.

Day 46: Growing Up in the Spirit

We should no longer be children, tossed to and fro and carried about with every wind of doctrine, by the trickery of men, in the cunning craftiness of deceitful plotting, but, speaking the truth in love, may grow up in all things into Him who is the head—Christ.
Ephesians 4:14-15

Grow in the grace and knowledge of our Lord and Savior Jesus Christ. To Him be the glory both now and forever. Amen.
2 Peter 3:18

Dear One,

Come, sit awhile with Me. You need say nothing; just acknowledge My presence that is with you.

My child, do not waste time on doubt and disbelief. These are the lies and the traps of the enemy. Recognize his ploys. Grow up in the Spirit. Do not bite the bait of the evil one. He knows which bait to use to get you to "bite." Question what it is that you feed on. Feed on truth and not on lies. Be cautious, not lazy. I have given you wisdom.

I love you, My child. I withhold no good thing from you. Receive life. Make good choices, and you will live a full life. Make foolish choices, and your life will be empty.

If you know what to do to be filled with My life, why choose the opposite?

Make space for life in the Spirit. Feed your spirit, and My life will flow out of you.

Day 47: Growth in Intimacy

And I will pray the Father,
and He will give you another Helper,
that He may abide with you forever—
the Spirit of truth, whom the world cannot receive,
because it neither sees Him nor knows Him;
but you know Him, for He dwells with you and will be in you. I will not leave you orphans;
I will come to you.
John 14:16-18

And this is eternal life, that they may know You,
the only true God, and Jesus Christ
whom You have sent.
John 17:3

However, when He, the Spirit of truth, has come, He will guide you into all truth; for He will not speak on His own authority, but whatever He hears He will speak; and He will tell you things to come. He will glorify Me, for He will take of what is Mine and declare it to you. All things that the Father has are Mine. Therefore I said that He will take of Mine and declare it to you.
John 16:13-15

To My Bride Who Waits,

You have come to Me in reluctant faithfulness. I see that you want to begin again. Beginning again is good—it is better than giving up and never starting again. There is a risk involved in coming to this virgin place of showing up and waiting to be impregnated with My

Word. You must trust My faithfulness, and not look at your unfaithfulness to Me. I am only looking at your showing up in prayer this time. My mercies are new every morning. I am not resentful.

You must know that when you do not show up or make time for Me, I am there for you. Even if you "stand Me up," I always stand by waiting for you to come aside with Me in the still, quiet place of prayer and prayerful listening. I speak in ways that you can hear. I do not intend to discourage you, but to encourage you to come aside with Me awhile. See that I am faithful.

In speaking to you in ways that you can hear and acknowledge, I am making this a positive time together, rather than a negative, frustrating time. I want to be heard just as much as you want to hear Me. There are many people, and they hear and see in different ways. Look around you with the understanding that I intend to be found, and that I want to be seen. I am available, and I desire connection with My creation. It is not My pleasure to frustrate those seeking Me. Believe that you do hear and see Me, rather than that you are defective in perceiving Me. You may be experiencing challenges, but this does not hinder you from reaching me. I am not limited by your limitations.

Remember, this is about a two-way relationship. I am called the Hound of Heaven. Does this sound like I am reluctant to be found? No, I pursue you fervently. I will always speak to you. The question is, will you always make the time to be available to listen to Me?

Look at all of your life and see Me with you. If you are blocked in one dimension, know that I am not limited in finding ways to reach you. You only need to recognize Me. When did your heart leap? When were you comforted? When did you feel at home? Look for My footprints, as they may look differently than you thought they would appear. I can walk through walls, and I can pierce the darkness. Watch and see what I can do in your life.

Day 48: Reach for Him

O Lord, You have searched me and known me.
You know my sitting down and my rising up;
You understand my thought afar off.
You comprehend my path and my lying down,
And are acquainted with all my ways.
For there is not a word on my tongue,
But behold, O Lord, You know it altogether.
You have hedged me behind and before,
And laid Your hand upon me.
Such knowledge is too wonderful for me;
It is high, I cannot attain it.
Psalm 139:1-6

O God, You are my God;
Early will I seek You;
My soul thirsts for You;
My flesh longs for You
In a dry and thirsty land
Where there is no water.
So I have looked for You in the sanctuary,
To see Your power and Your glory.
Because Your lovingkindness is better than life,
My lips shall praise You.
Thus I will bless You while I live;
I will lift up my hands in Your name.
My soul shall be satisfied
as with marrow and fatness,
And my mouth shall praise You
with joyful lips.
Psalm 63:1-5

My Dearest One,

You delight Me with your words of love. I respond to your desire, and I will kindle your desire into a flame. Can we reach such intimacy, you ask? Can it be so between us? This is what you were created for, to be one with Me. Join Me, My lovely one. Reach out to Me tenderly, My dove, My young-at-heart Bride. Reach out to your Lord, who yearns for your love. It is I who calls you to Me. It is I, who put this boldness in your spirit to invite Me closer. I gave you such a desire for Me, which only I could fulfill.

I am drawing you to Me gently. Rest in My embrace. Be content with our union. It was designed to be so. This is not all there is. There is more, and you shall drink of it fully. Be satisfied with each portion I give to you. What you have is enough for the moment. Cherish the fullness of My love. Let Me lead you in a dance of intimacy with Me. I must lead and you must follow—not as a slave and a master, but as the Beloved and the Bridegroom.

Day 49: Stop Hiding

Abide in Me, and I in you.
As the branch cannot bear fruit of itself,
unless it abides in the vine, neither can you,
unless you abide in Me. I am the vine, you are the branches. He who abides in Me, and I in him, bears much fruit; for without Me you can do nothing.
John 15:4-5

And I will pray the Father,
and He will give you another Helper,
that He may abide with you forever.
John 14:16

Not that I have already attained, or am already perfected; but I press on, that I may lay hold of that for which Christ Jesus has also laid hold of me. Brethren, I do not count myself to have apprehended; but one thing I do, forgetting those things which are behind and reaching forward to those things which are ahead, I press toward the goal for the prize of the upward call of God in Christ Jesus.
Philippians 3:12-14

My Dear Betrothed,

You are spoken for and you are My intended one. I have an anointing for you with oils of gladness. Prepare yourself before entering the throne room. The throne room is beckoning to you, as I stand in it and call you to enter in. What will this be, this new call to come and see where I live?

Beloved, you have but only to take the first step. Step into My arms of love. They will embrace you as you journey closer to Me.

What do you ask of Me, My dear one? Do you want Me to draw you closer to Me? Do you want to be transparent to Me, or do you want to hide? To hide is to keep a part of you covered from the Bridegroom. Are you ashamed or afraid? Do you not trust Me with your heart? Are you afraid of being hurt? How intimate can we be? I will wait while you decide how safe I am. To be in transition is awkward. You do not know where you belong. Know that I know where you are and where you are going.

Come closer into the unknown. Stand in a place where you have yet to travel. Can you bare your soul to Me? Can you admit your deepest intentions and desires? Will you trust Me with your heart? Will you be willing to give up yourself, knowing that I will return to you who I know you to be? There is so much more to transformation. Draw closer to the purifying presence of My touch. My touch will define you, and it will forever leave an impression upon you.

You must leave behind the garments that formerly covered you, and with which you were familiar. I have other coverings for you, coverings that do not hide your beauty, but enhance it. You do not need as much to cover you as you thought you did.

It is safe in My presence, My Bride. Do not blush at what I see. I see you and I still call you to come closer, for there is more, much more to intimacy with Me. You must leave behind idols as you come closer to Me. Do you recognize your idols? I am a jealous God. I want nothing to keep us apart.

Day 50: Becoming Vulnerable

Draw near to God and He will draw near to you.
Cleanse your hands, you sinners; and purify your hearts, you double-minded.
James 4:8

Where shall I go from your Spirit?
Or where shall I flee from your presence?
If I ascend to heaven, you are there!
If I make my bed in Sheol, you are there!
If I take the wings of the morning
and dwell in the uttermost parts of the sea,
even there your hand shall lead me,
and your right hand shall hold me.
If I say, "Surely the darkness shall cover me,
and the light about me be night,"
even the darkness is not dark to you;
the night is bright as the day,
for darkness is as light with you.
For you formed my inward parts;
you knitted me together in my mother's womb.
I praise you, for I am fearfully and wonderfully made.
Wonderful are your works;
my soul knows it very well.
Psalm 139:7-14 ESV

My Dearest,

Come trusting to receive, and you will receive. Come prepared to be given to, and you will leave with gifts from the Giver of true gifts. I do not hide from you, but I am visible to you in the Spirit. Trust the revelations given to you. See with the eyes of the Spirit. Trust the

Spirit and what is revealed to you from the Spirit. Walking in the Spirit is different from your walk in the world.

Be anchored in Me and you will not lose ground. Look further inward. Listen deeply and you will hear Me. Practice cultivating the quiet. You do not need to do, but to be. Sit with your being-ness. Come within to the banquet. When you come to the banquet, clothe yourself with garments of praise and thanksgiving. Come as a vessel of quiet and gift Me with your presence. Your presence is what I desire most.

Day 51: Step Toward Him

The Spirit of truth, whom the world cannot receive, because it neither sees Him nor knows Him; but you know Him, for He dwells with you and will be in you. I will not leave you orphans;
I will come to you.
John 14:17-18

He will glorify Me, for He will take of what is Mine and declare it to you.
John 16:14

Delight yourself also in the Lord,
And He shall give you the desires of your heart.
Psalm 37:4

He who dwells in the secret place of the Most High
Shall abide under the shadow of the Almighty.
Psalm 91:1

My Beloved,

You, too, are My friend. I treasure your heart turned toward Me in loving gratitude. I appreciate your appreciation.

Turn to Me in expectation. I respond to you responding to My love. Do you hear that I listen for your response? I long for your desire. Do not grow cold in your love for Me. Remember to pursue Me. Does a lover not pursue His beloved? This is not considered work, but a natural response to love. Love is not work when it is motivated by delight. Without communication, love wanes. Do not forsake your first love. Am I not the object of your desire? I will teach you about bridal love. I desire a passionate love from My Bride. Do not allow your heart to grow cold with lethargy. Fan the flames of our love. Think of Me often. Delight yourself in Me, as I delight Myself in you. Embrace Me with your time. Spend time on Me, as I give time to you in return.

A bride does not need to be taught to think often of her beloved groom. You must do the same with Me. Be infatuated with the One who is infatuated with His Bride. Romance Me, My love. I desire to be desired. Ask Me how to please Me, and I will teach you how to do so. I am willing to lead you in the dance of intimacy. Do not be concerned that you may be awkward in My eyes. I am not difficult to please. The desire to please Me pleases Me. I realize this is new for you.

Just as you first haltingly spoke your prayer language, so begin to speak your love to Me. This love will grow as you grow it by your efforts to express it to Me. Risk feeling awkward in My eyes. I do not judge your attempts to love. I am pleased when you are obedient to

Me. Step out on new waters, My love. Be a Bride who is responsive in her love to her Groom.

Woo Me with your words. They are a love song to My heart. This frightens you, as this is a risk for you to love Me in a new way. Do not fear that you will fail. Trust that I am able to teach you the language of love. Rest in My love, My Beloved. Begin this day a new journey. There is no fear in love. I am gentle of heart toward you.

Day 52: Preparation

He who overcomes, I will make him a pillar in the temple of My God, and he shall go out no more. I will write on him the name of My God and the name of the city of My God, the New Jerusalem, which comes down out of heaven from My God. And I will write on him My new name.
Revelation 3:12

Let us be glad and rejoice and give Him glory,
for the marriage of the Lamb has come,
and His wife has made herself ready.
Revelation 19:7

Husbands, love your wives, just as Christ also loved the church and gave Himself for her, that He might sanctify and cleanse her with the washing of water by the word, that He might present her to Himself a glorious church, not having spot or wrinkle or any such thing, but that she should be holy and without blemish.
Ephesians 5:25-27

Dearest One,

Behold, I come to you in love. I am your Lover and you are My Bride. Let Me prepare you for the bridal feast. Come, sit beside Me as we celebrate our love. Lean on Me, My Beloved, as I speak to you.

My dearest one, you must know of My presence. I am with you always. I will supply what you need. I will be your source and your strength. I will speak to your heart in a language heard only by you, and I will speak in a language of love. You have only but to listen and you will hear Me, My Beloved.

I will dress you in garments made of love. They will reflect the Giver of the gifts. I will dress you in an identity of one chosen in and by love. I will adorn your hair in sunlight and radiance. I will put slippers of strength upon your feet.

Day 53: Come Closer

When I remember You on my bed,
I meditate on You in the night watches.
Because You have been my help,
Therefore in the shadow of Your wings I will rejoice.
My soul follows close behind You;
Your right hand upholds me.
Psalm 63:6-8

The LORD your God in your midst,
The Mighty One, will save;
He will rejoice over you with gladness,
He will quiet you with His love,
He will rejoice over you with singing.
Zephaniah 3:17

For though we walk in the flesh, we do not war according to the flesh. For the weapons of our warfare are not carnal but mighty in God for pulling down strongholds, casting down arguments and every high thing that exalts itself against the knowledge of God, bringing every thought into captivity to the obedience of Christ,
2 Corinthians 10:3-5

My Bride,

Open your heart to My speaking to you, My Beloved. Receive what I say to you, as one would receive rare jewels. My speaking to you is not rare, because the Creator does commune with His created ones. I ask you to receive My words at the communion table of your heart. Receive. Partake. Carry within you that which I have given to you. Know that you are Mine, and that I am yours.

You are My Bride and I draw you closer to Me. Do you not yet know that I am close by? Why do you doubt that you are chosen by Me? Is it that you discern by your feelings alone and not by faith in who I am and in what I say to you? Will silence cease to make us one? Will you wander around looking for Me, or will you know that I am with you, even in the silence? Will you press into My presence whether you sense Me near or not?

I know that you feel alone and forsaken, yet you keep turning to Me in prayer. This is what I love and receive as bouquets of flowers at My feet. Come closer. Do not fear. Enter in. You do not need heady manifestations, but only loyal devotions to Me. This is a stretching of your love for Me, when you love and pray when I seem hidden from you.

I am ever present and ever faithful, My fair one with the longing heart that only I can satisfy. Do not grow weary or despair, for I am with you always. Sit with Me in quiet stillness, even when your mind is racing. This is only a stage of pruning away of fleshly desires for satisfaction. Come to Me unencumbered, with no agenda and no expectations. Bring only yourself. You can do no more and I will do no less than promise to be waiting expectantly for you.

I await your sacrifice of love upon the altar of My presence. I am with you in the chambers of your heart. That is our special hiding place where we meet in the Spirit and the flesh does not detect us, but believes that nothing is happening. The flesh is deceiving, but the Spirit sees. I will give you a spiritual vision—a vision to see what I see. Until then, look with new eyes of faith. This time apart is a honeymoon for us, where I get to feed you. Allow me to feed you in My own special way, My Bride. Do not insist on what others are consuming. Your journey is your journey, not another's. We have had many blissful memories, but this is a time for a different level of love. Will you trust My love and not look longingly at how I love another? Remember, there are stages of growth. The stages are not meant to punish you, but to draw you to a new level. Do not resist the process as it is truly in answer to your heart's desire.

I am preparing My Bride, who must change garments in order to come and follow Me. Do not wear clothes of mourning for what once was and appears to be lost. Instead, joyfully wear the garments that I give you, knowing that I am pleased by what I am doing in you. I keep you apart for Myself. You are not cast off, but in preparation. Be in the waiting room of Love.

Day 54: The Narrow Path

It shall come to pass
That before they call, I will answer;
And while they are still speaking, I will hear.
Isaiah 65:24

...but, speaking the truth in love,
may grow up in all things
into Him who is the head—Christ—from whom the whole body, joined and knit together by what every joint supplies, according to the effective working by which every part does its share, causes growth of the body for the edifying of itself in love.
Ephesians 4:15-16

But the fruit of the Spirit is love, joy, peace, longsuffering, kindness, goodness, faithfulness, gentleness, self-control. Against such there is no law. And those who are Christ's have crucified the flesh with its passions and desires. If we live in the Spirit, let us also walk in the Spirit.
Galatians 5:22-25

Dearest Child,

I am here at our meeting place in the quiet. In the quiet I will renew you. Come, be with Me in stillness. Be still and know that I am the ever-present God. I am reachable, but the world believes that I am unreachable. They have settled for a lie. Do not sell out truth for the lies of the world. Dare to walk in truth. You will be a step apart from others, who walk according to the ways and the wiles of the world. Come over to the side of the Spirit, and continue walking in truth.

Walking in the Spirit will not always be popular. You will see and hear disapproval. Fear not—I am with you, and I am on your side. You do not need everyone's approval, you only need My approval. Fear not what the world thinks of you. The world has lost its way. My people follow where I lead. The path is narrow, and not all will follow. Come, follow Me as I lead you on the road home. Home has been your destination all along. You are in the world, but not of the world. Be comforted by this, as you are not lost, but walking in the Spirit.

Take time to listen to Me as I guide you. I will refine you until you are as pleasing to Me as fine gold. You are never alone, even when you feel most lost and forsaken. Know that I am at your side. Be still and come to Me, and I will give you refreshment. In My presence there is peace. In My presence there is safety. Come and receive all that I have for you.

Day 55: Growth in the Spirit

When I was a child,
I spoke as a child,
I understood as a child,
I thought as a child;
but when I became a man,
I put away childish things.
1 Corinthians 13:11

For this reason we also,
since the day we heard it,
do not cease to pray for you,
and to ask that you may be filled
with the knowledge of His will in all wisdom
and spiritual understanding;
that you may walk worthy of the Lord,
fully pleasing Him, being fruitful in every good work
and increasing in the knowledge of God...
Colossians 1:9-10

Coming to Him as to a living stone, rejected indeed by men, but chosen by God and precious, you also, as living stones, are being built up a spiritual house, a holy priesthood, to offer up spiritual sacrifices acceptable to God through Jesus Christ. Therefore it is also contained in the Scripture, "Behold, I lay in Zion a chief cornerstone, elect, precious, and he who believes on Him will by no means be put to shame." Therefore, to you who believe, He is precious; but to those who are disobedient, "The stone which the builders rejected has become the chief cornerstone," and "a stone of stumbling and a rock of offense." They stumble, being disobedient to the word, to which they also were appointed. But you are a chosen generation, a royal priesthood, a holy nation, His own special people, that you may proclaim

the praises of Him who called you out of darkness into His marvelous light; who once were not a people but are now the people of God, who had not obtained mercy but now have obtained mercy.
1 Peter 2:4-10

Dearest,

Behold, I am here with you. As you listen, you will hear Me speak to you. You are My Beloved, and I behold your spiritual beauty. I see beyond what you see. I see your hunger and your frustrations. I see your need for relationship with your Savior.

Keep coming to Me. Do your best, and that will be pleasing to Me. I love to be sought. I want you to be at peace in My presence. In My presence is rest, and that is why you sometimes slumber in prayer. In My presence is safety. You are not too complicated for Me, dear one. I know you intimately. I see beyond what you see. I do not have My back turned to you. Indeed, I show you favor. Grow in My loving presence. Sit with Me, and allow Me to work in your heart. Will you trust Me to do what needs to happen in your life? Will you trust when you cannot see? Will you trust the One who is hidden? I am more real than your thoughts and your vision. Allow Me to be in charge. I am trustworthy. Growing in the Spirit is seeing in faith what is there in spiritual reality. Entrust yourself to the Trustworthy One.

Keep coming closer. Do not grow discouraged by lack of experiences. Invest in relationship with Me. What is unseen must by faith become your reality and your foundation. Declare the truth to yourself and to Me. Build a healthy house in the Spirit. Dwell in that place with Me. You will grow, and you are growing.

See with eyes of faith. Sow into your faith. Lean into Me. I will take you all the way home. Your home is in Me. I am a sure foundation. I am the chief cornerstone and I am the Way. Come follow Me. Come and see where I live. Enter in, My child. Come home to your Father. I love you, and I am patient. I will help you. Will you be helped?

Day 56: He Calls You Beloved

Behold what manner of love the Father has bestowed on us, that we should be called children of God! Therefore the world does not know us, because it did not know Him. Beloved, now we are children of God; and it has not yet been revealed what we shall be, but we know that when He is revealed, we shall be like Him, for we shall see Him as He is.
1 John 3:1-2

Beloved, let us love one another, for love is of God; and everyone who loves is born of God and knows God. He who does not love does not know God, for God is love.
1 John 4:7-8

Therefore, as the elect of God, holy and beloved, put on tender mercies, kindness, humility, meekness, longsuffering...
Colossians 3:12

Beloved One,

I call you Beloved. Can you receive the endearment? Do you hear the tenderness in your name? Let the name rest upon your lips. Savor it. Beloved, I hold you in esteem when I name you as such. Your name reflects the love of the One who gives you this name, and this name also reflects your identity.

Rest in love, My Beloved. Dare to change your heart to receive this good news. The One who created the heavens created you. The One who fashioned the earth fashioned you. As I remember such details of the flowers and the birds, would I not remember you? I know you intimately. Can you accept being known by your Creator? Step into your name. Embrace your identity. Arise and walk in love. Lean into My presence as I lead you.

Day 57: He Calls You By a New Name

The Gentiles shall see your righteousness,
And all kings your glory.
You shall be called by a new name,
Which the mouth of the LORD will name.
Isaiah 62:2

And you, being dead in your trespasses
and the uncircumcision of your flesh,
He has made alive together with Him, having forgiven you all trespasses, having wiped out the handwriting of requirements that was against us, which was contrary to us. And He has taken it out of the way, having nailed it to the cross.
Colossians 2:13-14

Wash me thoroughly from my iniquity,
And cleanse me from my sin.
Psalm 51:2

My Dearest,

You are not bad. Your actions were wrong. You looked for solutions apart from Me, and this is sin. Sin is bad, but you are not.

I am your Redeemer. I redeem what was lost. I have brought you to a new season. You are a new person. Do not drag around your old wineskins and then try to fit into them. You are a new creation in Christ Jesus. I reflect who you are. Remember your name, My desirable one.

I speak to you because you are Mine, My Beloved. Do not hide in your old identity, when I have called you by a new name. Look what I have done! Rejoice, for this is a new day. The Lord reigns. Sin has lost its power. Isaiah 40:1-2 says, “Comfort, comfort My people, says your God. Speak tenderly to Jerusalem; tell her that her sad days are gone and her sins are pardoned. Yes, the Lord has punished her twice over for all her sins.”

Day 58: He Calls You Royalty

But you are a chosen generation,
a royal priesthood, a holy nation,
His own special people,
that you may proclaim the praises of Him
who called you out of darkness
into His marvelous light...
1 Peter 2:9

Blessed be the God and Father
of our Lord Jesus Christ, who has blessed us
with every spiritual blessing in the heavenly places in
Christ, just as He chose us in Him before the foundation
of the world, that we should be holy and without blame
before Him in love, having predestined us to adoption as
sons by Jesus Christ to Himself, according to the good
pleasure of His will, to the praise of the glory of His
grace, by which He made us accepted in the Beloved.
Ephesians 1:3-6

Dearest Child of the King,

You are royalty. Embrace your beauty in the King's eyes. You are His beloved child, and upon you His favor rests. You are not of lesser value than others whose gifts look shiny and bright. The gifts that I have given to you do not pale in comparison. How could a King give a gift of little value? All the riches of the Kingdom are at My disposal.

Stand up. Do not walk in the shadows. Come into the light, for you are to be seen. I have glory to show forth in you. Stand erect. Do not hang your head in shame. I have chosen you amongst man. Called forth, chosen, appointed, and anointed are My words spoken over you. Beloved bride, child of the most high God, My delight, reflect the Father's love to My people. My call upon you has a purpose in the Kingdom. Choose this day to follow Me. Walk in My footsteps. I will lead you to paths of freedom.

Day 59: He Feeds Your Deepest Hunger

But Jesus told him, "No! The Scriptures say, 'People do not live by bread alone, but by every word that comes from the mouth of God.'"
Matthew 4:4 NLT

"You're blessed when you've worked up a good appetite for God. He's food and drink in the best meal you'll ever eat."
Matthew 5:6 MSG

"For the bread of God is He who comes down from heaven and gives life to the world."
John 6:33

Dearest,

Rest in Me and relax. When you feel an anxious desire to eat, center on Me. Relax. Read My Word. Center on Me, the Bread of Life.

I will calm your urges. I will satisfy your inner hunger. Your inner hunger is a hunger that no food can satisfy. Only My Word and My peace can satisfy you.

Call on My Name. My Name is a name above all names. I am the Wonderful Counselor, and I am the Redeemer. I will set you free from your bondages. Trust in Me, and in My Word. My Word is life. My Word will fill you. You will not hunger when you are in My Word. My

Word is not a little appetizer. My Word is the entire meal—it is all of the courses. Do not just pick daintily at My Word; devour it.

Allow My Word to become part of you—one with you. Even if you do not understand it, keep reading it. As you consume more of it, it will be easier to digest it the next time. My Word will dissolve into you, feeding your every cell and feeding your inner hunger, a hunger that only I can satisfy.

Come to Me and partake of the meal of Life, the meal of Salvation. Rest in My Word. Contemplate My love. Rest in a blanket of care, as My words lull your spirit in a peace that comes only from Me. I will cradle you in My arms. Nestle in My arms as I feed you.

Day 60: He Gives You a Voice

I can do all things through Christ
who strengthens me.
Philippians 4:13

For God has not given us a spirit of fear,
but of power and of love and of a sound mind.
2 Timothy 1:7

"Have I not commanded you? Be strong and of good courage; do not be afraid, nor be dismayed, for the LORD your God is with you wherever you go."
Joshua 1:9

The LORD is my light and my salvation;
Whom shall I fear?
The LORD is the strength of my life;
Of whom shall I be afraid?
Psalm 27:1

Dearest,

Do not fear what man can do to you. Do you not know that I am with you always? Your voice must be spoken in order to be heard. I did not intend your voice to be put on mute. Start with one statement at a time. You do not have to climb a mountain the first try.

Day 61: He Knows Your Name

But as many as received Him, to them He gave the right to become children of God, to those who believe in His name: who were born, not of blood, nor of the will of the flesh, nor of the will of man, but of God.
John 1:12-13

The thief does not come except to steal, and to kill, and to destroy. I have come that they may have life, and that they may have it more abundantly. I am the good shepherd. The good shepherd gives His life for the sheep. But a hireling, he who is not the shepherd, one who does not own the sheep, sees the wolf coming and leaves the sheep and flees; and the wolf catches the sheep and scatters them. The hireling flees because he is a hireling and does not care about the sheep. I am the good shepherd; and I know My sheep, and am known by My own. As the Father knows Me, even so I know the Father; and I lay down My life for the sheep.
John 10:10-15

Because he has set his love upon Me,
Therefore I will deliver him;
I will set him on high,
Because he has known My name.
Psalm 91:14

Dearest One,

You are My noble one. Live up to your name. Live as royalty, as indeed you are such. Beloved of the Father, child of a King. Royal blood runs in your veins. Hold up your head. Walk in your identity in Christ.

Live to give honor to the King. Your ransom was costly, and the King agreed to pay it with the blood of His Son.

I will write a letter on your heart. Rise up. You were created to bring glory to the King. Step out of the shadows, My fair one. Cast your own shadow. Today is a new day. Reflect your Maker's glory.

Delight yourself in Me, My love, as I delight Myself in you. Sing songs of gratitude over Me. Gratefulness is a prayer offered to Me. Remember He who gives you all things. Train yourself to see My handprints upon your life. I appreciate appreciation. With a heart full of gratitude, you will experience joy. In the joy of the Lord is your strength. You are stronger than you realize. I am stretching your borders. Lean into Me as I direct your path.

Day 62: He Sets You Apart for Him

I do not pray that You should take them out of the world, but that You should keep them from the evil one. They are not of the world, just as I am not of the world. Sanctify them by Your truth. Your word is truth. As You sent Me into the world, I also have sent them into the world.
John 17:15-18

And do not be conformed to this world, but be transformed by the renewing of your mind, that you may prove what is that good and acceptable and perfect will of God.
Romans 12:2

Do not be unequally yoked together with unbelievers. For what fellowship has righteousness with lawlessness? And what communion has light with darkness? And what accord has Christ with Belial? Or what part has a believer with an unbeliever? And what agreement has the temple of God with idols? For you are the temple of the living God. As God has said: "I will dwell in them and walk among them. I will be their God, and they shall be My people." Therefore "Come out from among them and be separate, says the Lord. Do not touch what is unclean, and I will receive you. I will be a Father to you, and you shall be My sons and daughters, says the LORD Almighty."
2 Corinthians 6:14-18

My Dearest,

You are My righteousness. I clothed you in the blood of My Son. I designed you to be exactly the way you are. Do not attempt to take the chisel from the Master Sculptor. You are being designed into My creation. You were not created for the world, but for Me to use in the world.

Please your Master Creator and not the world. Choose the side you will be on. Stand with Me, and I will guide you. Stand with Me, and I will strengthen you. Stand with what I say, and you will blossom.

If you stand by the world and its values, you will be empty, for the world can destroy you. I am the Truth. Plant yourself in eternal truth, and not in transitory values. Do not cling to pleasing others to get approval, as approval is a false god. Step down from the altar of approval and belonging to something you were created for. Risk looking inward. Listen for My voice, and I will speak. I will tell you who you are. Listen to My truth and not to the world with its distorted beliefs. Do not listen to those who need you to be a certain way for their own peace of mind.

Do not alter or bury who I say you are in order to get false approval. False approval is hollow, and it will not heal you. Only the truth can heal you. Risk standing in truth with Me over standing in the truth of another's reality and needs. You are dishonoring both yourself and others when you are not true to who I have created and am creating.

I am not finished with you. This is not because you are so flawed; it is because I am continuing a good work designed by Me for you. It takes time and willingness to create. There are stages of pliability in which I can work, and there are seasons of resting and waiting. Do not grow impatient, as I know how much time I need, and your days are numbered in My Book.

Trust the process. I know what is best. I will neither rush it to please you, nor will I delay it to punish you. You are mine, and I love you. I know best what you need. I do not see flawed and damaged goods when I see you. I see you from eyes of love. I believe in you. I have broken into your heart of doubt and planted seeds of hope and belief. You are not too complicated for Me.

Day 63: He Treasures Your Prayers

Seek the LORD and His strength;Seek His face evermore!
1 Chronicles 16:11

...pray without ceasing...
1 Thessalonians 5:17

Be anxious for nothing, but in everything by prayer and supplication, with thanksgiving, let your requests be made known to God...
Philippians 4:6

Beloved,

I treasure your words to Me. Can you receive this truth? As parents treasure their child's works of art, so do I treasure your words spoken to Me. I enjoy your company. Share with Me your thoughts during the day and in the evening. Reach Me with your heart. Do not place Me in one or two categories of the day, but expand your conversation with Me to include your entire day. I do not expect long prayers, but I do enjoy a turning of your heart toward Me throughout the entire day and evening. I am not a hard taskmaster. I ask that you think of Me frequently. Turn your heart toward Me, as I turn My heart toward you. You are always on My mind.

Rest in love, as Love rests in you. You are My Beloved. Allow this to soften your heart toward Me. I am approachable. Are you? As you place more of your heart in My presence, there will be more of My heart in yours. Receive My love. Allow it to transform you. Be mine, My love. Be mine. I am yours for all eternity.

Day 64: Hearing God's Voice

You shall walk after the LORD your God and fear Him, and keep His ommandments and obey His voice; you shall serve Him and hold fast to Him...And all these blessings shall come upon you and overtake you, because you obey the voice of the LORD your God.
Deuteronomy 13:4, 28:2

I can of Myself do nothing. As I hear, I judge; and My judgment is righteous, because I do not seek My own will but the will of the Father who sent Me.
John 5:30

...while it is said: "Today, if you will hear His voice, do not harden your hearts as in the rebellion."
Hebrews 3:15

My Child,

Hear Me speak to you, My lovely one. Develop your ear by time spent listening to Me. Be obedient to My Words.

Can you trust Me more than you trust your doubts? Whose ear do you have—Mine, or the lies? Do you really believe that I live in you and that I speak to those who belong to Me? It is wise to be disloyal to beliefs that turn you away from Me and from hearing My voice. It is time to know that I am here for you and in you. Stop the struggle and embrace the truth. You do know Me and you do hear from Me. This is the good news to cling to, and not your doubts and disbeliefs.

Talk to Me more, and you will hear from Me more often. I cannot speak to you when your ear plugs are in. Doubt and disbelief are spiritual earplugs. Get rid of them, regarding My speaking to you. Do not limit Me, and do not limit what I can say to and through you by thinking that I can't or won't speak to you. Look at Me and not at others.

Day 65: His Indwelling Presence

I will put My Spirit within you
and cause you to walk in My statutes,
and you will keep My judgments and do them.
Ezekiel 36:27

If you had known Me,
you would have known My Father also;
and from now on you know Him
and have seen Him.
John 14:7

But you are not in the flesh but in the Spirit, if indeed the Spirit of God dwells in you. Now if anyone does not have the Spirit of Christ, he is not His.
Romans 8:9

Beloved,

Behold, I speak of a truth to touch the hearts of My wounded ones. I am a personal God, and I dwell in the tents of My people. I am neither on top of a mountain, nor am I in the wind, but I dwell within each creation who asks Me to come into his or her heart. Can you believe this truth, that I come and dwell within you? No matter how many or how few people are in your life, know that I dwell within you.

If you had company living in your house, would you go next door to visit, and ignore the visitor within your home? Do not neglect the One who loves you the most. Remember, I dwell within you, and I desire a covenant relationship with you. You are mine and I am your God.

I am a God to love and adore, but please do not forget Me in your busyness. Remember where I dwell, and come within to visit Me. Be in relationship with Me. Draw from the wealth of riches within. Do not go running around begging for scraps when there is a banquet awaiting you within. Come and feast. Drink of My choice wine. Feast on the Paschal Lamb.

Run to Me and not from Me. It is easier to acquire information than to take the time to be in relationship with Me. Taking the time for Me is hard for your flesh, as your flesh wants to move and receive, and to gather more things. What you need to do is to tame the flesh by coming within and keeping this time with Me, whether or not you feel like it. The flesh must bow to Me, that My Spirit may work in you with abundance. Step out of the world as you know it, and enter the world of the Spirit. Come and sit with Me, as I teach you. Behold He who loves you. Enter into My throne room.

Day 66: His Love Heals You

He heals the brokenhearted
And binds up their wounds.
Psalm 147:3

But He was wounded for our transgressions,
He was bruised for our iniquities;
The chastisement for our peace was upon Him,
And by His stripes we are healed.
Isaiah 53:5

Then your light shall break forth like the morning,
Your healing shall spring forth speedily,
And your righteousness shall go before you;
The glory of the LORD shall be your rear guard.
Isaiah 58:8

Beloved,

I delight in you. You are Mine forever. Rest in Me. You are safe in my healing arms of love. I can heal you in ways you never imagined. Trust in Me. You have felt passed over and that you were too difficult a case. Nothing surpasses my ability. I am not without recourse. Watch and see what I can do. I am not too good to be true. I am Truth and I am willing.

Your spirit is hearing Me speak to you. I am yours forever. You do not know how good I am to you. Your name is not passed over. I see you. Your healing will come and you will know a new freedom. My love for you is eternal. Come closer. You are safe with Me. My love will heal you from the inside out. You are a new creation. Do not run from Me, but run to Me.

Day 67: His Love is Eternal

For I am persuaded that neither death nor life,
nor angels nor principalities nor powers,
nor things present nor things to come,
nor height nor depth, nor any other created thing,
shall be able to separate us from the love of God which is in Christ Jesus our Lord.
Romans 8:38-39

But You, O Lord, are a God full of compassion, and gracious, Longsuffering and abundant in mercy and truth.
Psalm 86:15

Dearest Beloved,

My love for you is eternal. Rest in the security of My faithful love towards you, My dearest. Rest in your identity as the Beloved. My love for you will never be fickle. You can trust My heart and My nature. I am Love and Love remains faithful.

Our conversations may change, but I will never change. After all this time you still struggle with My goodness towards you. Rest assured that I am for you, and not against you. My heart is vast and deep. I am reliable, My love, as none other. Challenge the reliability of your doubts. Drink from My love and be satisfied.

Day 68: His Love is Healing

He heals the brokenhearted
And binds up their wounds.
Psalm 147:3

"Fear not, for I am with you;
Be not dismayed, for I am your God.
I will strengthen you,
Yes, I will help you,
I will uphold you with My righteous right hand."
Isaiah 41:10

"Come to Me, all you who labor
and are heavy laden,
and I will give you rest.
Take My yoke upon you and learn from Me,
for I am gentle and lowly in heart,
and you will find rest for your souls.
For My yoke is easy and My burden is light."
Matthew 11:28-30

Dearest One,

Regardless of how much you love Me, I love you more. My love is more than you can ever imagine. If you could experience the depth of My love, you would experience divine ecstasy. This is what Heaven will be like—a love that is given and fully received. For now, simply know that you are loved. This love is not based upon performance; it is freely given to you.

Do not put such high expectations upon yourself to be more than you are. You can be more after you appreciate yourself as you are. Until then, expecting more from yourself is futile. Love yourself as you are. Appreciate who you are. More will follow through love than through expectations.

My love calls forth the best in My people. My love allows you to become who you truly are. A narrow vision of yourself only restricts. See with eyes of possibility and potential. You are a gift, and you are gifted. I do not see you as less than others and a failure. My dear one is good, and you have much to offer. Stop chastising the one whom I love. It is hard to grow when you are at war with yourself. Call a truce. Be for, and not against, yourself. Sit with Me daily and I will come closer to you. I am the fullness for which you hunger.

Day 69: Hunger for the Lord

One thing I have desired of the LORD,
That will I seek:
That I may dwell in the house of the LORD
All the days of my life,
To behold the beauty of the LORD,
And to inquire in His temple...
When You said, "Seek My face,"
My heart said to You, "Your face, LORD, I will seek."
Psalm 27:4, 8

As the deer pants for the water brooks,
So pants my soul for You, O God.
My soul thirsts for God, for the living God.
When shall I come and appear before God?
Psalm 42:1-2

My Dearest,

What do you desire more than anything else? You desire your Beloved One to be in relationship with you. This is the cry of your heart, and I call it the desire for divine union with the One who created you from His own breath and from a desire for you.

Did you know that you were so desirable? I have desired you for such a time as this, My precious one. It is I who call to you, beckoning you to come closer. When you feel this, it comes to you as a deep longing. When you experience this longing, you interpret it to mean that you have lost something, or even that you never had it to begin with. In fact, I am calling you and drawing you closer yet.

Do not be afraid and do not lose heart, but instead rejoice in that you are indeed called and chosen. I have not forsaken you. I am with you. Look no further, for you are found and not lost. I see your heart.

Do not grow weary of the journey to Me. There is much more to experience. You are with Me, and you are coming to Me. Can you accept this? There is more, and this is a mystery—this is faith. You will never have all that you want, for I have given you a hunger for more of Me, and this requires much prayer time in My presence. Can you say yes to what will satisfy this hunger?

I do not expect the impossible from you, so do not fear that our love must be tedious times together, never quite reaching the goal. What I am telling you is that this hunger for more is good. Allow it to lead you to a deeper union with Me. I call you according to your capacity to give and to receive love. I already know where you are, and where you can be. Do not feel the pressure to perform, but instead feel encouraged to come closer, My beloved one. Our relationship is intimate, and it must not be diminished by comparisons to My relationships with others.

What I give to others in no way takes away from you; that is only your perception. Let Me interpret for you, for My eyes see without hindrance, and what I see is love. Look at what we have and not at what others have, for this is the key to happiness. Appreciate what is before you. You are not put on a meager ration of My presence; only your belief in this could make it appear so.

Your belief in Me must be expanded. I challenge you to become who I have always known you to be. Be pleased and not impatient with your progress, as progress takes time, and all time is in My hands.

Day 70: In Challenging Times

But may the God of all grace,
who called us to His eternal glory by Christ Jesus, after you have suffered a while,
perfect, establish, strengthen, and settle you.
1 Peter 5:10

Therefore, having been justified by faith,
we have peace with God
through our Lord Jesus Christ,
through whom also we have access by faith
into this grace in which we stand,
and rejoice in hope of the glory of God.
And not only that, but we also glory in tribulations,
knowing that tribulation produces perseverance; and perseverance, character; and character, hope. Now hope does not disappoint,
because the love of God has been poured
out in our hearts by the Holy Spirit
who was given to us.
Romans 5:1-5

The righteous cry out, and the LORD hears,
And delivers them out of all their troubles.
The LORD is near to those who have a broken heart,
And saves such as have a contrite spirit.
Psalm 34:17-18

My Child,

Although you have suffered much pain, your identity is not as a sufferer. Pain does not get to name who you are. The identity to claim is that of My beloved child. You are an overcomer, and you are victorious. The afflictions and the experiences do not get to name you. I call you by name, and you are named by Me alone. Do not exchange names. The name that I gave you is your true identity. Identify yourself with truth. Focus on your character as an overcomer in Christ.

Hold fast to what I say. Do not get sidetracked by powerful emotions, or by a painful affliction. Remember who you are. Take your focus off the infirmity, and place it on the One who holds all life together. I am the One who sustains your life. Come to the well of your sustenance. Drink freely. Come often. Abide in Me, and I will abide in you. My nature holds a wealth of resources for My children. Come feast on My richness. You are a privileged people who bear My name. You are a chosen people, a royal priesthood.

Rise up from your circumstances. Look to the One who created you to be more than your circumstances. Rise up, victorious one. Look into My eyes and see who you are. You are more than a conqueror. You are a city built on a hill. Allow My light to illuminate this city. Reach out in My name with My love. Tell the people that I live for them. Draw them home, those who have been lost and forsaken. It is for these that I have died, that none should be lost. Look beyond your life and see My lost ones around you.

Day 71: In Seasons of Waiting

Wait on the LORD;
Be of good courage,
And He shall strengthen your heart;
Wait, I say, on the LORD!
Psalm 27:14

But those who wait on the LORD
Shall renew their strength;
They shall mount up with wings like eagles,
They shall run and not be weary,
They shall walk and not faint.
Isaiah 40:31

Show me Your ways, O LORD;
Teach me Your paths.
Lead me in Your truth and teach me,
For You are the God of my salvation;
On You I wait all the day.
Psalm 25:4-5

Dearest Beloved,

Rejoice, for you are favored. You have not felt favored, and you have believed that others were favored and that you were not favored. I judge differently than man does. You are included. I have plans that include you. Do not grow weary of waiting upon Me. You are somebody of value.

Be at peace. I know where you are. My plans for you are good plans. Trust in Me at all times. You are not forsaken. This is a year of the favor of the Lord, even though this year has seemed anything but the favor of the Lord. See through My eyes of love. Do not grow weary of waiting. There will be a shift. Wait for My move. I will raise you to a new level. Be prepared. The One who lifts your head is here.

Day 72: In Times of Darkness

Why are you cast down, O my soul?
And why are you disquieted within me?
Hope in God, for I shall yet praise Him
For the help of His countenance.
Psalm 42:5

...who, contrary to hope, in hope believed,
so that he became the father of many nations, according
to what was spoken,
"So shall your descendants be."
Romans 4:18

Now may the God of hope fill you
with all joy and peace in believing,
that you may abound in hope
by the power of the Holy Spirit.
Romans 15:13

Dearest One,

Do you believe it when I say "dearest one"? Can you fathom the depths of love I have for you, My dearest one? You were created in Me and by Me from a burning desire for you to be. What I conceive of is good. What I desire is purely rooted in my love and will.

Do not think that I could ever regret creating someone. I know what I want, and I know who I want. You are who I want, and you were who I wanted. Do not allow your thoughts to tell you the opposite of the truth.

I knew the depths to which you could go, and I want you to fill those depths with My presence and with My Word. Read life into your darkness. Speak hope and truth unto yourself. Bring good news to the one who needs it the most—yourself. Do not allow your thoughts to ramble aimlessly and dangerously. Bring your thoughts back to truth, hope, and faith. Do not give free rein to your mind, as your mind has a path of its own. Corral your mind within certain safe areas, and when it strays, bring it "home" to truth and safety. Do not let your mind lead you; you lead your mind. When the mind is set on darkness, it will dig a pit. When the mind is set on what I say, the mind will be set free. Do not box yourself in; instead, free yourself by what I say to you. Allow My words to make you walk, then run.

Do not choose chains when you can have freedom. I have come to set you free from your chains. Do not put on the chains I have loosed. All of this takes time. From the depths, I will raise you up. You have only but to look up. Look at Me, and not at the chains of your circumstances. Hope in Me and you will not falter. I will loosen the grip of darkness from your mind. Give Me time, and trust where I will lead you. You were created for much more than this. Believe Me, and not your feelings, thoughts, and circumstances. I will set your mind free, but first you have to recognize that you have been a prisoner of your thoughts. Speak My name to your thoughts. Speak truth to the chains, and they will be loosed.

Day 73: In Trials and Tribulations

In this you greatly rejoice,
though now for a little while,
if need be, you have been grieved by various trials...
1 Peter 1:6

...strengthening the souls of the disciples, exhorting them to continue in the faith, and saying, "We must through many tribulations enter the kingdom of God."
Acts 14:22

These things I have spoken to you, that in Me you may have peace. In the world you will have tribulation; but be of good cheer, I have overcome the world.
John 16:33

Dearest,

Find your joy in the present day, and in what is currently before you. You will not find it in what is not here. It will not be found in what could have or should have happened yesterday or in the future. Today is My gift to you. Find the treasure hidden in this day. Look for the blessings given to you.

When the day set before you is dark and your heart is heavy with grief, look to the One who is the lifter of your head. Look to the One who is closer than a brother. Lean your heart onto Mine, and I will comfort you. I am a refuge to be sought in the storms and the joys of life. I am forever faithful. I am your Shepherd, who is never lost or confused. Seek Me even when you feel forsaken by Me. I am here with you, as I cannot lie, nor can I betray My nature. You are not lost to Me. I see you, My child. I see your needs and desires. Do not lose heart—I am near.

I am the joyful one who rejoices in His children. I rejoice in your desires for more of Me. I do not call you greedy or unappreciative. I call you My hungry one who knows that there is more to be given. All riches are to be found in Me. Search for Me first, before you search for My favors. Sit at My feet and be in My presence. Do not think that you are left out or deprived of better things. My timing is perfect. My plan is divine. I am building trust in you. Trust that I am here for you, and that I am providing for you all that you need for this season of your life. You have a place at My table, and this is indeed good news.

I have given you an anointing that will be fulfilled. You do not need to figure it out. I know the time. Do not pull against the reins, like a horse determined to lead the way. Submit to Me. I know the way, as I am the Way.

Day 74: You Are Victorious

...that the genuineness of your faith, being much more precious than gold that perishes, though it is tested by fire, may be found to praise, honor, and glory at the revelation of Jesus Christ...
1 Peter 1:7

And He said to me, "My grace is sufficient for you, for My strength is made perfect in weakness." Therefore most gladly I will rather boast in my infirmities, that the power of Christ may rest upon me.
2 Corinthians 12:9

Have I not commanded you? Be strong and of good courage; do not be afraid, nor be dismayed, for the LORD your God is with you wherever you go.
Joshua 1:9

Dearest One,

You will rise from all of your circumstances that now seem to hold you captive. You will stand with Me in victory. Nothing that has befallen you will take you down in defeat, for you shall stand and walk away from these places of pain and loss to the other side. Believe that this is truth to rely on. Believe more in this than in the evidence of your circumstances. This is the fork in the road. Which side will you stand on—the evidence of circumstances, or what I tell you as I speak to your heart?

Listen. Hear the truth that will save you. You are not defined by your fiery trials. No, your trials only empower you in Me. Walk in truth. Hold onto it as to a life preserver in stormy seas. Look to who holds the life preserver to you. I am the Life Preserver and the Life Restorer. I am Life in the fullest, and I am the Way—the way out and the way through.

I am here, and I will not leave you as you are refined in the fire of trials. You are bigger than the trials that could change your focus and direction. Do not get out of the fire and run away. Stay and be tested. Wait for the results to be printed upon your character. You will grow and stretch to beyond your image of who you believed yourself to be. I will provide your reflection for you. Gaze into My presence, and see what I will show you. I will remove from your eyes that which keeps you from seeing truth. I will give you My eyes to see what is really there. Do not fear. It is I walking on the waters with you. Keep looking at Me, and you will not sink. I am here for you, My child. You are able to accomplish the tasks I set before you.

Day 75: Endurance

Blessed is the man who endures temptation; for when he has been approved, he will receive the crown of life which the Lord has promised to those who love Him.
James 1:12

Beloved, do not think it strange concerning the fiery trial which is to try you, as though some strange thing happened to you; but rejoice to the extent that you partake of Christ's sufferings, that when His glory is revealed, you may also be glad with exceeding joy.
1 Peter 4:12

My Child,

You are not being punished, but prepared. Can you endure the fiery furnace? Will you stay where I have placed you? I know what is in store for you, and your life holds many riches and promises. I am faithful. Will you believe in My goodness? Will you believe that there is more ahead for you, not less? Will you have hope and not despair? I have so much for you, and you will live to see it. I am not finished with My work in you. Do not give up.

Day 76: He Is With You

No temptation has overtaken you except such as is common to man; but God is faithful, who will not allow you to be tempted beyond what you are able, but with the temptation will also make the way of escape, that you may be able to bear it.
1 Corinthians 10:13

My brethren, count it all joy when you fall into various trials, knowing that the testing of your faith produces patience. But let patience have its perfect work, that you may be perfect and complete, lacking nothing. If any of you lacks wisdom, let him ask of God, who gives to all liberally and without reproach, and it will be given to him. But let him ask in faith, with no doubting, for he who doubts is like a wave of the sea driven and tossed by the wind. For let not that man suppose that he will receive anything from the Lord; he is a double-minded man, unstable in all his ways.
James 1:2-8

My Child of Hope,

Your hope in Me will not leave you forsaken. I am One who will never leave My Bride waiting at the altar. You are not deserted at this trying time in your life. Just because you feel lost, uncertain, and abandoned, do not believe that this is spiritual truth. I am aware of all that happens or does not happen. I do not overlook you and your needs and desires. My will is not to break your heart and leave you lonely at this or any time in your life. My will for you will always be love. I am not standing at a distance watching you, as one does an experiment in a laboratory.

I am with you in all the trials and fires you face. I never ask you to face what I personally did not face. I know what you are made of, even when you are blind to it yourself. You believe you need some things that are not meant for you, or which you have outgrown. You are in the process of growing into something much bigger, yet you cling to a former way of being. You are ready for more, and I am giving you more. All is not as it seems to be. Can you sit with the discomfort of changes, and wait upon Me as I work within you? Listen to what is around you. Look within and find Me.

Stand firm in faith in Me. I will not fail you, but I will uphold you. Do not panic as the fire is turned up. I know what it takes to get the results that I desire for you. Watch and see who you are. You are a new creation.

Day 77: The Battle Is Won

...rejoicing in hope, patient in tribulation,
continuing steadfastly in prayer...
Romans 12:12

Therefore we also, since we are surrounded
by so great a cloud of witnesses, let us lay aside every
weight, and the sin which so easily ensnares us,
and let us run with endurance the race
that is set before us, looking unto Jesus,
the author and finisher of our faith,
who for the joy that was set before Him
endured the cross, despising the shame,
and has sat down at the right hand
of the throne of God.
Hebrews 12:1-2

Beloved,

Rise up, Beloved of the Father. It is not too late. Fight the fight for emotional health. The battle has already been finished. Fight to stand in the victory that was won for you. Do not allow the enemy's thoughts to become your thoughts. Be vigilant. Discern. You are more than a conqueror. The past is past. Do not visit the past as if to glean from it hidden jewels. I will bring to you jewels from the refining of your life. You have what you need to resist your feelings.

Day 78: Trust His Plan

For I consider that the sufferings of this present time are not worthy to be compared with the glory which shall be revealed in us.
Romans 8:18

Therefore we do not lose heart.
Even though our outward man is perishing,
yet the inward man is being renewed day by day. For our light affliction, which is but for a moment,
is working for us a far more exceeding and eternal weight of glory, while we do not look at the things which are seen, but at the things which are not seen. For the things which are seen are temporary, but the things which are not seen are eternal.
2 Corinthians 4:16-18

Dearest One,

Hope in Me and you will not be disappointed. Believe what I have told you shall come to pass. I am not short of memory. I remember you. My timing is just on time.

You are being prepared by being emptied. Do not fear the process of letting go, so you may be filled with more of Me. This time apart is not meant to hurt you. When I set you apart for a season, it is not punishment. I have a plan. Use this time wisely. Solitary time is not meant to depress you, but to impress upon you who has your ear and your heart.

Your life has revolved around your friendships, but not around your friendship with Me. I desire to be first in your life. I do not want to be last place, or "if there is time left over" place. Time with Me needs to be regular. Think of Me more. I think of you always. I will hold you close to Me and I will not let you fall backward. Believe that I know what I am doing in your life.

Day 79: The Risen One

And we know that all things work together for good to those who love God, to those who are the called according to His purpose...Who shall separate us from the love of Christ? Shall tribulation, or distress, or persecution, or famine, or nakedness, or peril, or sword? As it is written: "For Your sake we are killed all day long; we are accounted as sheep for the slaughter." Yet in all these things we are more than conquerors through Him who loved us. For I am persuaded that neither death nor life, nor angels nor principalities nor powers, nor things present nor things to come, nor height nor depth, nor any other created thing, shall be able to separate us from the love of God which is in Christ Jesus our Lord.
Romans 8:28, 35-39

And lest I should be exalted above measure by the abundance of the revelations, a thorn in the flesh was given to me, a messenger of Satan to buffet me, lest I be exalted above measure. Concerning this thing I pleaded with the Lord three times that it might depart from me. And He said to me, "My grace is sufficient for you, for My strength is made perfect in weakness." Therefore most gladly I will rather boast in my infirmities, that the power of Christ may rest upon me. Therefore I take pleasure in infirmities, in reproaches, in needs, in persecutions, in distresses, for Christ's sake. For when I am weak, then I am strong.
2 Corinthians 12:7-10

Dearest One,

The Lamb of God is risen indeed in your heart. Rejoice at the news of resurrection. Let not your heart be weary or heavy laden, for the Lamb has risen indeed. Bring your burdens to the Lamb. Lay them at My feet. Let Me fill you with My love, as I am the Risen One. Your burdens are not forever. No, you will also one day rise. For the Risen Lamb has risen, and pain will one day die.

Do not give up on your journey. Trust in the One who calls your name. Keep walking your walk, regardless of the circumstances before you. You will rise from your circumstances, because of the Risen One. For the Risen Lamb is with you, and you never walk alone. Lean upon My gentle mercy. Receive what I have for you. I will assist you in your journey. Never fear, never fear. I call you to walk beside Me. You will never be alone. The Risen Lamb is the Resurrection, and you belong to Me.

Rest in My holy presence. Be restored in My love. Trust in the direction I take you. Trust the journey you are on. Come follow Me to victory. Come walk your walk beside Me. The Risen One is calling, and you will not be alone.

Trust My eyes to lead you, even when you are lost in your pain. I know the way to victory. I know what you cannot see. Use My eyes to see, My dear one. I will gladly show you the way. Lean upon the Merciful One, and begin again this day. Do not forget that I will lead you where you could not walk alone, along paths especially chosen for you. On the other side, you will know victory. There are victories every day.

Follow Me, oh follow Me. I will walk with you. Lean upon Me, and I will show you the way. The way out is through. You have been equipped for the journey.

Day 80: He Has More for You

Many are the afflictions of the righteous,
But the LORD delivers him out of them all.
Psalm 34:19

Why are you cast down, O my soul?
And why are you disquieted within me?
Hope in God, for I shall yet praise Him
For the help of His countenance.
O my God, my soul is cast down within me;
Therefore I will remember You
from the land of the Jordan,
And from the heights of Hermon,
From the Hill Mizar.
Psalm 42:5-6

The LORD God is my strength;
He will make my feet like deer's feet,
And He will make me walk on my high hills.
Habakkuk 3:19

Dearest Beloved,

Rejoice, the Lord is with you. Rejoice, I am within. Alleluia. Even unto the end of time, I will be with My people. I am bound to you through love and desire. Come closer, come closer. There is so much more to be discovered. Let Me reveal Myself to you. Let Me draw you closer to My heart of love. Sit in My presence, and just be with Me. I will speak to you heart to heart. I will draw you to Me with strings of love. Will you trust My love?

I want so much for you, but you quake in fear, lest I take some treasure from you. You clutch with hope and desperation to your treasures. You cling to them as your security. They will not give you lasting comfort. They will only bind you to them, and not to the lasting peace I desire for you. To be in My will is to be in peace, even in the midst of a storm. I have so much for you, yet you continue to cling to those objects of satisfaction that have outlived their purpose.

You turn to food, as does one who turns to a life preserver to keep him from sinking into the sea. You do not need that support. Step out and see the support I have for you. My presence is sweeter than any food and any amount of overeating meant to soothe you and to distract you. Risk letting go into My love. Take that leap into the unknown, and find Me there. What you fear will not overcome you.

Do not compare your abilities to another. Each journey is different. There is nothing to compare. If another gets to where you want to be before you do, rejoice. This is hope that is offered you, not something to taunt you with your failure at not arriving sooner. You may take longer to arrive. You are not to judge. Only I know the reason behind all struggles. Do not despair. To each there is a season. Your season is coming.

Day 81: Instructions in Love

And now, Israel, what does the LORD your God require of you, but to fear the LORD your God, to walk in all His ways and to love Him, to serve the LORD your God with all your heart and with all your soul...
Deuteronomy 10:12

So he answered and said, "You shall love the LORD your God with all your heart, with all your soul, with all your strength, and with all your mind," and "your neighbor as yourself."
Luke 10:27

Beloved, let us love one another, for love is of God; and everyone who loves is born of God and knows God. He who does not love does not know God, for God is love.
1 John 4:7-8

Dearest Beloved,

Delight yourself in Me, as I delight Myself in you, My lovely one. You are My beloved Bride, My joy.

Do not worry about how you feel in regard to your love for Me. Love wanes, but continue in our love. Just keep saying yes to Me. I will never fail you. Realize how much I love you, My dear one. Continue to do what you can do, as I continue My work in you. Keep giving Me your heart through daily choices. This is your faith walk of love.

Behold, your Bridegroom is at the door knocking. Will you come to the door in obedience? Show up in faith. I am preparing you. You must step into new dimensions of faith for this level of relationship. I am indeed here with you. Keep believing. Keep pressing onward. If you could see what I see, you would easily press on toward the prize.

I am the One who calls you to keep coming closer. You only keep coming toward One who is there, not one who is not there. I am present and you are in relationship with the unseen One. This is not in your mind, but in your spirit. Do not grow weary, nor be discouraged. Focus on the prize—everlasting life with the One whom you pursue. Your love is what I desire. Choose love. Remain faithful.

Day 82: Be His Original

And Thomas answered and said to Him, "My Lord and my God!" Jesus said to him, "Thomas, because you have seen Me, you have believed. Blessed are those who have not seen and yet have believed."
John 20:28-29

For we dare not class ourselves or compare ourselves with those who commend themselves. But they, measuring themselves by themselves, and comparing themselves among themselves, are not wise.
2 Corinthians 10:12

For the kingdom of heaven is like a man traveling to a far country, who called his own servants and delivered his goods to them. And to one he gave five talents, to another two, and to another one, to each according to his own ability; and immediately he went on a journey...

After a long time the lord of those servants came and settled accounts with them. So he who had received five talents came and brought five other talents, saying, "Lord, you delivered to me five talents; look, I have gained five more talents besides them." His lord said to him, "Well done, good and faithful servant; you were faithful over a few things, I will make you ruler over many things. Enter into the joy of your lord."

He also who had received two talents came and said, "Lord, you delivered to me two talents; look, I have gained two more talents besides them." His lord said to him, "Well done, good and faithful servant; you have been faithful over a few things, I will make you ruler over many things. Enter into the joy of your lord."

Then he who had received the one talent came and said, "Lord, I knew you to be a hard man, reaping where you have not sown, and gathering where you have not scattered seed. And I was afraid, and went and hid your talent in the ground. Look, there you have what is yours." But his lord answered and said to him, "You wicked and lazy servant, you knew that I reap where I have not sown, and gather where I have not scattered seed. So you ought to have deposited my money with the bankers, and at my coming I would have received back my own with interest. Therefore take the talent from him, and give it to him who has ten talents."

For to everyone who has, more will be given, and he will have abundance; but from him who does not have, even what he has will be taken away. And cast the unprofitable servant into the outer darkness.
Matthew 25:14-15, 19-30

Dear One,

I did not make you on an assembly line. You are unique. Do not try to copy another. Be the individual that I created you to be. I am growing you. Be content with who you are—I am. People have gifts, but their gifts are not their identity. I am their identity. I hold the mirror to reflect to them who they are. Rely upon Me and what I say. Others will reflect your identity based upon their perception of you, which could be flawed. You are in a safe place to grow, even if you feel inadequate. The soil in which I have placed you will produce growth. Fight against the grasshopper mentality. Do not look at others—look at Me. Be encouraged.

Day 83: Invest in Time with God

I am the true vine, and my Father is the vinedresser. Every branch in me that does not bear fruit he takes away, and every branch that does bear fruit he prunes, that it may bear more fruit. Already you are clean because of the word that I have spoken to you. Abide in me, and I in you. As the branch cannot bear fruit by itself, unless it abides in the vine, neither can you, unless you abide in me. I am the vine; you are the branches. Whoever abides in me and I in him, he it is that bears much fruit, for apart from me you can do nothing.
John 15:1-5 ESV

But when you pray, go into your room and shut the door and pray to your Father who is in secret. And your Father who sees in secret will reward you.
Matthew 6:6 ESV

Now as they went on their way, Jesus entered a village. And a woman named Martha welcomed him into her house. And she had a sister called Mary, who sat at the Lord's feet and listened to his teaching. But Martha was distracted with much serving. And she went up to him and said, "Lord, do you not care that my sister has left me to serve alone? Tell her then to help me." But the Lord answered her, "Martha, Martha, you are anxious and troubled about many things, but one thing is necessary. Mary has chosen the good portion, which will not be taken away from her."
Luke 10:38-42 ESV

Dearest Beloved,

The time that you give to Me is a treasured gift. I enjoy getting to know you intimately.

I give you choices, and you get to decide how to spend the life that I give to you. Will you invest in eternity, or will you buy into the things of this world? Choose wisely, My love. Spend your time in the school of love. Sit at My feet, and I will teach you things that matter to My heart.

Cleanse your mind from the effects of the world as you sit in My presence. I will loosen your attachments to the ungodly things of this world. You can invest more time in relationship with Me. When you do this, I give you more in return. How I love to surprise you with blessings.

My love, do not keep Me waiting for you. I long for you, My Beloved. Do not grow weary of the journey toward Me.

Day 84: Jesus Is Always With You

For I am sure that neither death nor life, nor angels nor rulers, nor things present nor things to come, nor powers, nor height nor depth, nor anything else in all creation, will be able to separate us from the love of God in Christ Jesus our Lord.
Romans 8:38-39 ESV

Therefore I tell you, do not be anxious about your life, what you will eat or what you will drink, nor about your body, what you will put on. Is not life more than food, and the body more than clothing? Look at the birds of the air: they neither sow nor reap nor gather into barns, and yet your heavenly Father feeds them. Are you not of more value than they?

And which of you by being anxious can add a single hour to his span of life? And why are you anxious about clothing? Consider the lilies of the field, how they grow: they neither toil nor spin, yet I tell you, even Solomon in all his glory was not arrayed like one of these. But if God so clothes the grass of the field, which today is alive and tomorrow is thrown into the oven, will he not much more clothe you, O you of little faith? Therefore do not be anxious, saying, "What shall we eat?" or "What shall we drink?" or "What shall we wear?"

For the Gentiles seek after all these things, and your heavenly Father knows that you need them all. But seek first the kingdom of God and his righteousness, and all these things will be added to you. Therefore do not be anxious about tomorrow, for tomorrow will be anxious for itself. Sufficient for the day is its own trouble.
Matthew 6:25-34 ESV

Behold, I stand at the door and knock. If anyone hears my voice and opens the door, I will come in to him and eat with him, and he with me.
Revelation 3:20 ESV

Dear Child,

My presence is always with you. Even when you do not recognize Me, I am present. Do not trust your earthly vision, as it will fail you. Ask for spiritual vision, that you might see the truth. Do not judge what is happening by what you see. If your vision is cloudy, it will only deceive you.

I am at work, even when all looks silent, dry, and inactive. I am moving. I do not need to reveal signs and wonders in order to be working in your life and in the life of your family. I work gently, and I wait to be invited. Nothing is beyond what I can do. No problem is too great for Me.

Learn to look with spiritual vision, vision that trusts when one does not see or feel. Trust that I am faithful to My promise never to leave you. Even in the dead silence of waiting, I am with you. It is hard to wait in the desert. Listen to the quiet. Listen to the waiting, as it has something to say to you. Not all pain is bad. Pain can be a teacher. You can learn from pain, once you quit struggling to avoid it.

Relax and hear what I have to say to you, regardless of what circumstances you find yourself in. If you find yourself in a prison, use that time to be with Me. Glorify Me the best that you can, and your chains will not cut you and keep you from life. Your outer chains cannot restrict your soul. Turn to Me and ask Me what you are to do. Your chains can be broken, as I have broken all chains and bondages.

Relax. Pray. Wait. Listen. You are not alone. Relax, and you will not go under in the struggle. It is when you thrash about in the waters of adversity that you go under. When you relax and breathe in My presence, you will have the peace and the ability to hear, think, and move in My Spirit. Do not thrash about wildly in your life, as one who has no rescuer from the angry seas. I am here. Trust Me. I know where you are. I never said that it would be easy, but I did say that I would not leave you orphaned. Do not forget who your Father is.

Do not become immobilized in your life. Keep moving. To move is to be alive. Waiting for Me to speak does not mean waiting to live. Use what I have given you. Do the best that you can do, knowing that I am He who stirs you, and I am He who says, "Arise and walk." Do not take a couple of baby steps and then sit down and wait for Me to say "walk" again. Keep moving. You can move as well as listen. You can wait by turning your heart to Me, and by turning your ears to My Spirit. Waiting does not mean lying by the road until I speak again. Pick up your mat and walk. I have given you strength. Use what I have given you.

Day 85: Jesus is Your Shelter

The Lord himself goes before you and will be with you; he will never leave you nor forsake you. Do not be afraid; do not be discouraged."
Deuteronomy 31:8 NIV

For in the day of trouble he will keep me safe in his dwelling; he will hide me in the shelter of his sacred tent and set me high upon a rock.
Psalm 27:5 NIV

Even though I walk
through the darkest valley,
I will fear no evil,
for you are with me;
your rod and your staff,
they comfort me.
Psalm 23:4 NIV

My Child,

Come to Me. I am your shelter from stress. I am your harbor from life's troubles. Dock in Me. I will feed you that which will connect you more firmly to My presence. I draw you to Me. Lean into Me. Feast upon Me. I am here waiting. I am longing for you to find in Me that which you have been searching for. When you are in Me you will see better, because you will see from My perspective.

Day 86: Jesus Is Your Truth

...and you will know the truth, and the truth will set you free.
John 8:32 ESV

In their case the god of this world has blinded the minds of the unbelievers, to keep them from seeing the light of the gospel of the glory of Christ, who is the image of God.
2 Corinthians 4:4 ESV

The natural person does not accept the things of the Spirit of God, for they are folly to him, and he is not able to understand them because they are spiritually discerned.
1 Corinthians 2:14 ESV

Dearest,

You are My Beloved. Rejoice in My favor. Release your insecurities to Me, as I can only reflect the truth to you. Look into the mirror of truth to receive your directions. How could I lie to you, as I am the Truth?

Find your identity in Me. You are who I say you are. Humans can only reflect what they can see, and they see only dimly.

You were meant to live in My kingdom. Walk as royalty. Think and speak as royalty. Does this not change your perspective?

You are going against the grain of Satan's intentions when you listen to your Creator. The enemy would have you believe that I do not speak to My children, and that My children cannot hear the voice of their Father. What a deception this is. Dare to believe the truth and rise above the lies of the enemy. When your experience has told you otherwise, you will need to take a leap of faith in order to align yourself to what I say to you. Dare to believe a different thought. See where life is. I am Life, and what I say to you brings life and not death.

Day 87: Jesus Loves the Brokenhearted

The Lord is near to those who have a broken heart,
And saves such as have a contrite spirit.
Psalm 34:18

"The Spirit of the Lord is upon Me,
Because He has anointed Me
To preach the gospel to the poor;
He has sent Me to heal the brokenhearted..."
Luke 4:18

And He said to me, "My grace is sufficient for you,
for My strength is made perfect in weakness."
Therefore most gladly I will rather
boast in my infirmities,
that the power of Christ may rest upon me.
2 Corinthians 12:9

My Child,

Your brokenness is not a lack, but it is a place of vulnerability. In your brokenness you are open to My fullness. In your weakness I am strong. Because of your lack, be sure that My power is at work in you and through you. Your brokenness is a vehicle through which I enter, and through which I work. Do not limit yourself because of your limitations, and do not think that I can only work in a vessel that is whole and polished. There is less of you when you come to Me in your need and in your lack.

I have come to heal the hearts of My brokenhearted. I come for those who have needs. Count yourself blessed, not scorned. The whole are few, whereas the wounded are many. It is to the multitude that I come and bring the good news of life. I am Life, and in Me you will be whole. In Me you will find rest, and in Me you will find answers. Seek Me, and you will find Me. Seek busyness, and you will reap unrest. I call you to come and see who I am. See how I love and whom I love. Walk with Me and love My lonely ones. See their hurting hearts. Look and I will show you the hearts of My people. Prepare yourself by prayer. Without prayer, you cannot see and you cannot help. With prayer all things are possible.

Believe what I say, and you will walk on the waters of your life with Me.

Day 88: Jesus Sets Captives Free

The Spirit of the Lord God is upon Me,
Because the Lord has anointed Me
To preach good tidings to the poor;
He has sent Me to heal the brokenhearted,
To proclaim liberty to the captives,
And the opening of the prison
to those who are bound;
To proclaim the acceptable year of the Lord,
And the day of vengeance of our God;
To comfort all who mourn,
To console those who mourn in Zion,
To give them beauty for ashes,
The oil of joy for mourning,
The garment of praise for the spirit of heaviness;
That they may be called trees of righteousness,
The planting of the Lord, that He may be glorified."
And they shall rebuild the old ruins,
They shall raise up the former desolations,
And they shall repair the ruined cities,
The desolations of many generations.
Isaiah 61:1-4

The Lord is not slack concerning His promise,
as some count slackness,
but is longsuffering toward us,
not willing that any should perish
but that all should come to repentance.
2 Peter 3:9

For though we walk in the flesh, we do not war according to the flesh. For the weapons of our warfare are not carnal but mighty in God for pulling down strongholds, casting down arguments and every high thing that exalts itself against the knowledge of God, bringing every thought into captivity to the obedience of Christ...
2 Corinthians 10:3-5

Beloved of the King,

Nothing is too complicated for Father God to heal. Nothing is beyond My range of expertise. I am not surprised or perplexed by mankind. I am God, and I am able and willing to reach down from the heavenlies and speak freedom to those in captivity. Some of those in captivity do not even know that they are held as captives. My Son has set the captives free.

Tell those in bondage that the Bondage Breaker is here, and that He is willing and able. Nothing is beyond His reach. Do not lose heart, for the One who reigns on high is here. I have overcome the dark one. I will mend the broken places, and I set the captives free in Zion.

Rise up, Jerusalem. Your borders will be enlarged. No longer will you be a captive city or a city in ruins. I speak restoration. I am the Repairer of the Breach. I speak freedom to you, captive Israel. Your time is at hand. Rejoice, for I have come to set you free. No longer will you be in exile, but you shall return to your city, and I shall rebuild it. Your walls will be restored. You shall be a fortress, and your gates shall be restored. Rise up, for the King of Glory is near. Freedom is near. Rejoice, for your healing is at hand. Your Redeemer lives, and so shall you live, and declare the goodness of God in the land of the living.

Recognize that the One who lives within you has the power to move mountains of doubt and disbelief. Are you ready to release them? They have protected you from disappointment. Will you trust in Me and in My goodness? All things are possible for those who believe. I have loved you with an everlasting love.

Day 89: Letting Go of Offenses

Be kind to one another, tenderhearted, forgiving one another, as God in Christ forgave you.
Ephesians 4:32 ESV

But I say to you, Love your enemies and pray for those who persecute you...
Matthew 5:44 ESV

"Be angry, and do not sin": do not let the sun go down on your wrath, nor give place to the devil.
Ephesians 4:26-27

My Child,

Do not hang onto the old things that hurt you, like sins and offenses. When you do this, I cannot cleanse you and bring the new things I have for you. Do not wrap yourself in old, shriveled things. Do not clothe yourself in death, like a tree that would gather up its old leaves and wrap them in bundles around itself, crowding out the new growth of leaves that I would bring in the spring.

You cannot give something away, like clothing that you leave at the curb to be picked up, and then run to the curb and bring it back into your house again before it is picked up. Your identity is not in old things and in old wounds. Your identity is in Me.

Write down all that has offended you that you still struggle with. Write it "out of you" and give it to Me to heal and to deal with. Do not keep it alive by reliving it over and over. Learn from it. Change and become more like Christ. Do a new thing by releasing the prisoner, which is not the offender, but yourself.

As you show mercy to the offender, you will be showing mercy to those parts of yourself that are capable of doing the same thing to others. Your home is not in dead wounds. Your home is in Me. I can bring life out of death, but first you must say goodbye to the dead things you have gathered around yourself. I have so much more for you than ashes. Ashes are not your clothing. I provide your garments for you. I will give you beauty for your ashes.

Day 90: Listen in the Quiet

And you will seek Me and find Me,
when you search for Me with all your heart.
Jeremiah 29:13

My son, if you receive my words,
And treasure my commands within you,
So that you incline your ear to wisdom,
And apply your heart to understanding;
Yes, if you cry out for discernment,
And lift up your voice for understanding,
If you seek her as silver,
And search for her as for hidden treasures;
Then you will understand the fear of the Lord,
And find the knowledge of God.
Proverbs 2:1-5

Dearest One,

Behold the truth and meditate upon it. Hold My words in your mind and in your heart. Find comfort and joy in them. Count on them, and allow them to be your foundation. Rest in My words, and renew yourself in them.

My words will wash away the effect of other words spoken in judgment and cruelty. My words will be a healing balm, soothing away a history of words that wounded your spirit.

Come to the well and drink freely. I call you to come and sit at the feet of Him who knows all. My Word to you is to come and follow Me. See where I live. Believe that I dwell within you. Run to Me and not from Me. Run into the shelter of My welcoming arms. Dare to believe the truth. Trust Me and not the deceiver, who comes but to rob and to destroy. Do not be loyal to his lies. Align yourself with Me, and you will stand. Give your ear to the prince of darkness, and you will falter and crumble. Only truth prevails. Draw near to the truth, and allow it to satisfy your deepest longing to belong and to be loved. Do not be fed by the father of lies. Drink from the living stream of life eternal.

You have chosen the better portion, and you have broken bread with truth. This is where your loyalty lies. Make your home in Me, as I will make My home in you. Do not be afraid to lean against Me. I am your strong tower, and I will not sway. I am your hiding place, and I will not betray you. I have given everything to you, and I have given everything for you. After all this, why would I turn from the one who seeks Me? I await My people's love. I desire their longing of their Savior.

I am a personal God and not a distant one. This is good news that remains a secret to many people. You have heard the truth and you know Me, even though you sometimes doubt what is true. Can you believe the truth? Does the truth frighten you? In order to accept the truth, you need to let go of the lies upon which you have built your house. Now I call you to start again. This is not punishment, but progress.

Take it one day at a time, and turn to Me with questions. I am your Teacher, and I will give you My Spirit to guide you.

Day 91: Look to the Lord

My son, do not forget my law,
But let your heart keep my commands;
For length of days and long life
And peace they will add to you.
Let not mercy and truth forsake you;
Bind them around your neck,
Write them on the tablet of your heart,
And so find favor and high esteem
In the sight of God and man.
Trust in the Lord with all your heart,
And lean not on your own understanding;
In all your ways acknowledge Him,
And He shall direct your paths.
Proverbs 3:1-6

For if anyone is a hearer of the word and not a doer, he is like a man observing his natural face in a mirror; for he observes himself, goes away, and immediately forgets what kind of man he was. But he who looks into the perfect law of liberty and continues in it, and is not a forgetful hearer but a doer of the work, this one will be blessed in what he does.
James 1:23-25

But we all, with unveiled face, beholding as in a mirror the glory of the Lord, are being transformed into the same image from glory to glory, just as by the Spirit of the Lord.
2 Corinthians 3:18

My Dearest,

Behold, I am your mirror of Truth. Look to Me for wisdom. I am Truth, and I cannot lie. There is no deceit in Me. Follow Me. I will not lead you astray. I will only point you in the direction of the Father. I am your compass. You are not lost, but found. Your safety relies upon trusting the trustworthy One.

Day 92: Make Time for Jesus

Be still, and know that I am God;
I will be exalted among the nations,
I will be exalted in the earth!
Psalm 46:10

Then He said, "Go out, and stand on the mountain before the Lord." And behold, the Lord passed by, and a great and strong wind tore into the mountains and broke the rocks in pieces before the Lord, but the Lord was not in the wind; and after the wind an earthquake, but the Lord was not in the earthquake; and after the earthquake a fire, but the Lord was not in the fire; and after the fire a still small voice.
1 Kings 19:11-12

Dearest One,

I speak to you in the quiet. Quiet is the realm of my communion with you. Be still and know that I am God. I am with you, and I am in you. I am the available Father who listens to His children, and who listens for His children.

Make space for intimacy, that intimacy may happen. Create an environment for intimacy, and you will experience moments of quiet union with the Father of Love. Keep holy the time you set apart for Me. I am the Faithful One who never forsakes you. I am dependable.

Depend on Me. Your ears will be trained for listening as you keep the silence by waiting upon Me.

My love is eternal, as I will love you for all eternity. Eternity begins today. Walk as one who is the Beloved of God. You are not an orphan. The fullness of God is at your disposal. Receive as one who is rich, and not as one who is impoverished. I give to you freely. Freely receive. Your Father has much to give to you.

Day 93: Make Wise Choices

A man's heart plans his way, But the Lord directs his steps.
Proverbs 16:9

My son, if you receive my words, and treasure my commands within you, So that you incline your ear to wisdom, and apply your heart to understanding; Yes, if you cry out for discernment, and lift up your voice for understanding, If you seek her as silver, and search for her as for hidden treasures; Then you will understand the fear of the Lord, And find the knowledge of God. For the Lord gives wisdom; from His mouth come knowledge and understanding; He stores up sound wisdom for the upright; He is a shield to those who walk uprightly; He guards the paths of justice, and preserves the way of His saints. Then you will understand righteousness and justice, equity and every good path.
Proverbs 2:1-22

Dearest One,

I await your listening and your availability to listen. Our time together brings life. Choose life. Align yourself with what I say, and you will have fullness of life. Do not accept whatever crosses your mind; discern your thoughts with diligence. Do not entertain your mind with that which is not entertainment. Choose wisely, and choose life, not death. The path you are on has many choices and forks. Choose wisely, and you will be wise.

I am willing to give you more—are you willing to receive it? Are you willing to sacrifice your down time with My Spirit in order to be refreshed and renewed? To grow in My Spirit requires dedication. Are you willing to let go of some things, that you may be open to receive something new? Put down lethargy and passivity, and be determined to reach for the more.

I have placed you in a church that you may grow spiritually. To grow requires sacrifice. Choose carefully. You do not need as much time in front of the television watching nothing of much value. You have other resources; use them. Do you want your flesh to increase, or do you want increase in your spirit? Drink from the well of living waters. I am willing to teach you. Choose to be teachable. The student must study. The student makes wise use of his or her time. This is not something you are unable to attain.

The Kingdom is within, and it is within your reach. Do you want Me to help you? Make new habits of availability, and you will learn. I will show you what you are to do. I am the Teacher. Avail yourself of the resource set before you. This is a new season. Step into the new. Embrace Me as I lead you.

Day 94: Make Wise Use of Your Time

And as it is appointed for men to die once,
but after this the judgment...
Hebrews 9:27

But seek first the kingdom of God and His righteousness,
and all these things shall be added to you.
Matthew 6:33

See then that you walk circumspectly, not as fools but as
wise, redeeming the time, because the days are evil.
Ephesians 5:15-16

Dearest Beloved,

You still doubt My desire to speak to you each day. Would not a lover speak daily to his beloved? How much more do I want to communicate with you, My Beloved. Each day is a fresh start, a new beginning in our love. Write upon each day the intentions of your heart toward Me. What sort of letter will you write, My love? It takes intention followed by effort to move forward. Imprint upon the day your heart toward Me. Time is the choice you make toward Me. How will you spend the time given to you? Time will one day run out for you, so make each day count. I am not a hard taskmaster. Follow where your heart leads. Will your heart lead to Me?

Day 95: Members of the Family of God

But as many as received Him, to them He gave the right to become children of God, to those who believe in His name.
John 1:12

Behold what manner of love the Father has bestowed on us, that we should be called children of God! Therefore the world does not know us, because it did not know Him. Beloved, now we are children of God; and it has not yet been revealed what we shall be, but we know that when He is revealed, we shall be like Him, for we shall see Him as He is.
1 John 3:1-2

...but if I am delayed, I write so that you may know how you ought to conduct yourself in the house of God, which is the church of the living God, the pillar and ground of the truth.
1 Timothy 3:15

My Child,

You belong to the family of God. No longer are you an outsider. You belong. Search no more for approval and belonging. What you seek is already available.

You were chosen—chosen to be born and chosen to be loved, regardless of what you said, did, or did not do. You cannot earn My approval. When you look into My eyes you will always see delight, as I delight in My creation. That which you long for already exists. You are worthy of love and approval.

Do not allow another's pain or opinion to devastate you, as they are only one person, and what they say or do reflects upon their experiences. Some people are limited in loving; that is their handicap. Do not define yourself according to another's limited perception of your behavior. Look at the bigger picture. You jump to embrace the pain as truth, when indeed, the pain was a lie. Love expands; lies restrict. Do not step in and accept that which limits, names, and defines you, when it does not come from truth and love.

Day 96: Mulch

I am the leaves of an earlier season of your life that have fallen to the earth. I am the leaves that defined you now becoming something new. I am richness of prior seasons being called to a different purpose—to enrich the ground of your foundation.

I become a source of nutrients—not seen, not measured, but yet valuable to the life source of the tree. This process of becoming mulch seems less grand than to be a leaf that gives shade and glorifies the tree. I want to hang on and to be that leaf, swaying in the wind, belonging to this lovely vital tree.

This is a season of my life. Like the caterpillar that goes into the cocoon, and then becomes a butterfly after a season of darkness, so am I called to trust in the process of life...to the rising and to the dying, and to the rebirth. When I submit to the process of life, death, loss, and rebirth, I can be part of a greater plan.

Help me, Lord, to willingly let go, to fall to the ground and settle into Your plan for my life, and to trust that life goes on and that I, too, shall go on. I am becoming more than I have earlier defined myself. Help me to let You define me as wholly Yours. Help me not to cling to where I found life so sweet, and not to resist Your touch to transform me beyond my previous identity.

May I be willing to be the donkey that carried You toward Your destiny. Help me to believe in the resurrection of new life, new purpose, and new seasons to experience Your divine life. It is not over yet; the song goes on. There is richness in the nutrients of the mulch oozing into the earth. Taste and see that there is still beauty within. Beauty comes from the ashes of mulch.

Help me to yield to You, my Lord, that I may become all that You intended me to become. Sing songs over my barrenness. Wake me up to Your glory. Wring out of me all that is fruitful. Use me up, before I am gone—all for Your glory.

It is not over. I still have more within me. Oh, mulch of my life, teach me your lessons, that I may embrace the plan of my destiny in Him who named me.

Day 97: My Word Is Your Foundation

Therefore whoever hears these sayings of Mine, and does them, I will liken him to a wise man who built his house on the rock: and the rain descended, the floods came, and the winds blew and beat on that house; and it did not fall, for it was founded on the rock.
Matthew 7:24-25

Now may the God of hope fill you with all joy and peace in believing, that you may abound in hope by the power of the Holy Spirit.
Romans 15:13

And immediately Jesus stretched out His hand and caught him, and said to him, "O you of little faith, why did you doubt?"
Matthew 14:31

Dearest,

An artist must first prepare his canvas before painting a picture. You must prepare for prayer by having quietness within you. The quietness comes from quiet prayer and time in My Word. You need to be more familiar with My Word, so that you recognize it when it is spoken. As My Word becomes more one with you, you will overflow with it.

Will you lay down the heavy veil of doubt and allow yourself to believe? To believe is to risk, to walk on the unchartered waters of your life. There is nothing wrong with discerning, but in discerning what I give to you, you paint yourself into a corner of doubt, disbelief, and fear. Dare to believe that I do speak to you and that I am moving in your life. Stop listening to the thoughts that cripple you and keep you stuck in the corner. It is time to come out of the corner of "stuckness" and enter a new walk of faith and belief. Give Me your doubts, as they have kept you paralyzed in a web, unable to go forward. Try something new. Change position to one that is secure in your relationship with Me. You are not an orphan, but My child. You are not lost, but found. Stop denying your heritage and your inheritance.

Day 98: On Being the Beloved

My beloved is mine, and I am his.
Song of Solomon 2:16

As for God, His way is perfect;
The word of the Lord is proven;
He is a shield to all who trust in Him.
Psalm 18:30

Do you not know that you are the temple of God
and that the Spirit of God dwells in you?
1 Corinthians 3:16

Dearest Beloved,

Get used to being called My Beloved. Does this name fit your nature? Emanate My love, My dear one. You are the Beloved of God. I bless you out of My goodness and mercy.

My love for you is everlasting. Rest in the confidence of My ever-present love. Do you not feel the joy of being loved? Do you receive being lovable in My sight? I am generous in My affection. Allow love to mold you into one of My choosing. I will fashion you with tenderness and grace. Am I not generous in My mercy?

Receive My plan for your life. Do I not know you best? I am all seeing. My vision is unquestionable. I make no mistakes. The time that I take to fashion you is determined by what I plan to do in your life. Do not second-guess Me. Will you trust My motives and desires? All that I do comes from good, and only good comes from what I do. I am trustworthy.

Do not grow impatient with the process. My timing is just on time. Do not rush or try to delay it, as I am in charge of your life. I give you free will, and you can step in and derail My plans for you. Surrender to My will for your life. Trust Me, My love, as I want what is best for you. You may not see down the road and around the corners of your life, but I can do so. Do not second-guess Me.

A horse, once broken, yields to its rider's desires. Allow yourself to yield to My desires. You fear losing freedom, but when you yield to My will, you will gain freedom. This is how it is in the kingdom of God—you lose to gain, and you submit to gain freedom. I will teach you many things along the way, My child. The journey you are on is rich with possibilities. Surrender to My capable plan. Come closer to Me, as I am safe.

Day 99: Your Identity in Christ

...being confident of this very thing, that He who has begun a good work in you will complete it until the day of Jesus Christ...
Philippians 1:6

And we know that all things work together for good to those who love God, to those who are the called according to His purpose.
Romans 8:28

having predestined us to adoption as sons by Jesus Christ to Himself, according to the good pleasure of His will...which He made to abound toward us in all wisdom and prudence...
Ephesians 1:5, 8

Beloved One,

You are the one I call Beloved. Your name is recorded in My book. I rejoice when you treasure what I have given to you. I appreciate appreciation.

Rise up and walk in the fullness of your calling. Move in the anointing that I have given to you. You are not empty, but full of My Spirit. I am working in you to bring about My will for you. Can you trust Me to move at the appointed time? You feel that your time to serve Me has expired. Your expiration time is not up. I know what I am doing.

You have taken some turns that have set you back, but even setbacks are of no surprise to Me. I am in charge. I am still able to do more than you have ever dreamed or imagined. Rise up, child of the King. You are qualified for great things in My Father's kingdom. Your brokenness is not a barrier to Me.

Day 100: Abiding

For You formed my inward parts;
You covered me in my mother's womb.
I will praise You,
for I am fearfully and wonderfully made;
Marvelous are Your works,
And that my soul knows very well.
My frame was not hidden from You,
When I was made in secret,
And skillfully wrought
in the lowest parts of the earth.
Your eyes saw my substance, being yet unformed.
And in Your book they all were written,
The days fashioned for me,
When as yet there were none of them.
Psalm 139:13-16

For we are His workmanship,
created in Christ Jesus for good works,
which God prepared beforehand
that we should walk in them.
Ephesians 2:10

My Dearest,

I call you "dearest." I value you, Beloved one. You have been found in Me. You have a home and an identity. My Son has called you into the light of His presence. Stand in His presence. This is your shelter. You are safe in His presence. Walk in truth, as I am the Truth. Move in the presence of the One who calls you forth. Your life is not your own. You are not a prisoner of the father of lies.

Discern his interference, but do not live in fear, for you are free by the blood of the Lamb. Risk walking in the truth of your identity. What do you have to lose? I love to see you move in the freedom that was won for you by the cross. Do not be deceived by the deceiver.

Rejoice, Jerusalem, for today is a new day. Your Beloved is yours. He holds you securely in His arms. Walk in faith and in freedom. Do not carry yesterday with you. I am your home and your promise. Abide in Me, as I abide in you. Be restored in My love. My love is yours, freely given by Me.

Day 101: You Are Chosen

And you, being dead in your trespasses and the uncircumcision of your flesh, He has made alive together with Him, having forgiven you all trespasses, having wiped out the handwriting of requirements that was against us, which was contrary to us. And He has taken it out of the way, having nailed it to the cross.
Colossians 2:13-14

Blessed be the God and Father of our Lord Jesus Christ, who has blessed us with every spiritual blessing in the heavenly places in Christ, just as He chose us in Him before the foundation of the world, that we should be holy and without blame before Him in love...In Him also we have obtained an inheritance, being predestined according to the purpose of Him who works all things according to the counsel of His will...
Ephesians 1:3-4, 11

My Beloved One,

You are blessed by the One who names you. Walk in that truth. Receive the blessing and put down the lies. What you have believed is that you are empty, rejected, and an outcast. Instead, you are named, chosen, called, and filled with the life of the One who calls you by name.

Walk in dignity, My love, for you are loved. Do not reject your Lover and embrace the deceiver.

Rise up, My Beloved. Come alive. Wake up. You are meant for great things in My kingdom. Look around you. Speak life to those I send to you. Come forth. Do not rest in the shadows. Come forth and live in the light. Lean into My presence. Be filled. As you give it away, you will receive more. Your cup will overflow. That which you give away will come back to you, pressed down, overflowing.

Blessed is the one who reflects her Maker. You are rich in blessings. Rise up and reach out. Today is a new day. The Lord lives. Blessed be the name of the Lord. Glorify His name upon the earth.

Day 102: Be Secure in His Love

I have been crucified with Christ; it is no longer I who live, but Christ lives in me; and the life which I now live in the flesh I live by faith in the Son of God, who loved me and gave Himself for me.
Galatians 2:20

Therefore, if anyone is in Christ, he is a new creation; old things have passed away; behold, all things have become new.
2 Corinthians 5:17

Dearest,

I see into the corners of your heart. You are known to Me. Nothing about you is a mystery to Me. You have always been known to Me.

Do not hide in shame. Shame is not a good hiding place. When you hide in shame, you are denying who you are and who I am. I am He who sees. You are my child. Your deeds are already seen and known, so why hide, as Adam and Eve did? I see you, and you are good. I call you good. Do you want to dispute your Maker? You will always sin, because you are not yet perfected. Look at Me, and look at what I say to you.

If you must hide, hide in the security that you are my beloved. My delight is in you. Receive the truth and let that adorn you. Do not hide under the rags of your sinfulness, when I gave you the beauty of My righteousness. Look at where you are standing.

Stand in the security of My love. Do not seek the shade of offenses. Sins and offenses are not places of life. Turn from the past to the present.

Do not become ensnared by comparisons. Comparisons are a trap. When you visit your past sins and camp out there, you become imprisoned by the sin. The sins were forgiven. Rest in forgiveness.

Day 103: Your Worship Pleases the Lord

Praise the Lord!
Praise God in His sanctuary;
Praise Him in His mighty firmament!
Praise Him for His mighty acts;
Praise Him according to His excellent greatness!
Praise Him with the sound of the trumpet;
Praise Him with the lute and harp!
Praise Him with the timbrel and dance;
Praise Him with stringed instruments and flutes!
Praise Him with loud cymbals;
Praise Him with clashing cymbals!
Let everything that has breath praise the Lord.
Praise the Lord!
Psalm 150:1-6

Serve the Lord with gladness;
Come before His presence with singing.
Psalm 100:2

Oh come, let us sing to the Lord!
Let us shout joyfully to the Rock of our salvation.
Let us come before His presence with thanksgiving;
Let us shout joyfully to Him with psalms.
For the Lord is the great God,
And the great King above all gods.
In His hand are the deep places of the earth;
The heights of the hills are His also.
The sea is His, for He made it;
And His hands formed the dry land.
Oh come, let us worship and bow down;
Let us kneel before the Lord our Maker.
Psalm 95:1-6

Dearest One,

How I love to hear you worship Me. I inhabit the place of your praises. I am drawn to your praise as metal to a magnet. Your spirit is refreshed as you bless Me.

Worship Me more often. Grow yourself by praising Me. You get to choose how often to do this. A sacrifice of praise will be rewarded. Do not underestimate the power of loving praise. More happens spiritually when you praise than you can comprehend. Make room for praise and gratitude. This produces a sweet aroma in your spirit. I am drawn to this sweetness.

Am I worth the time to glorify Me? Come closer. This is an invitation. Will you accept it?

Day 104: Overcoming Insecurity

...do not be anxious about anything, but in everything by prayer and supplication with thanksgiving let your requests be made known to God. And the peace of God, which surpasses all understanding, will guard your hearts and your minds in Christ Jesus. Finally, brothers, whatever is true, whatever is honorable, whatever is just, whatever is pure, whatever is lovely, whatever is commendable, if there is any excellence, if there is anything worthy of praise, think about these things. What you have learned and received and heard and seen in me—practice these things, and the God of peace will be with you.
Philippians 4:6-9 ESV

There is no fear in love, but perfect love casts out fear. For fear has to do with punishment, and whoever fears has not been perfected in love.
1 John 4:18 ESV

For those who live according to the flesh set their minds on the things of the flesh, but those who live according to the Spirit set their minds on the things of the Spirit. For to set the mind on the flesh is death, but to set the mind on the Spirit is life and peace. For the mind that is set on the flesh is hostile to God, for it does not submit to God's law; indeed, it cannot. Those who are in the flesh cannot please God. You, however, are not in the flesh but in the Spirit, if in fact the Spirit of God dwells in you. Anyone who does not have the Spirit of Christ does not belong to him. But if Christ is in you, although the body is dead because of sin, the Spirit is life because of righteousness. If the Spirit of him who raised Jesus from the dead dwells in you, he who raised Christ Jesus from the dead

will also give life to your mortal bodies through his Spirit who dwells in you.
Romans 8:5-11 ESV

My Dear One,

I call you My dear one, My fairest of the fair. I chose you long ago, and I have never changed My mind. You are My chosen one, though you doubt your cherished role in My kingdom.

Do you know that I know the thoughts and desires of your heart? I hear your cries and your moaning in the nighttime of your soul. Do not lose heart. Open up your heart in anticipation of My favor to you. My favor upon you is already decided; it is not to be won or lost. It is, and it shall be as I declare it to you.

Do not navigate your spiritual journey by your feelings. Chart your journey upon the words of the One who is unchangeable. Chart your journey by My desired will for you. Listen and lean toward Me. Yield to My perfect will. Do not depend upon your plan, with your time schedule for its unfolding. Give Me your desires and plans in return for My plans and desires. Submit to Me out of love, not fear. How can a bride cower in the presence of her groom and still love him from a place of freedom? No, I ask you to step into a place of trust. Can you take that leap of faith into My arms? Will you trust that I will not withdraw My arms from you? I am not fickle, and I am not subject to changes of heart. I am ever faithful. Do not look through eyes of fear. Instead, look to My eyes only, and I will show you the way.

Take the next step toward Me, and I will take the next step toward you. I give you free will, and I await the exercise of that free will toward Me. A feeble attempt is better than no attempt. Do not choose to feed a starving Spirit by means of the flesh. Flesh begets flesh. Spirit begets spirit. Choose by the Spirit, and your flesh will be the size it needs to be. Grow in the Spirit, not the flesh.

Day 105: Partake of His Word

All Scripture is given by inspiration of God,
and is profitable for doctrine, for reproof, for correction,
for instruction in righteousness,
that the man of God may be complete, thoroughly
equipped for every good work.
2 Timothy 3:16-17

Your word is a lamp to my feet
and a light to my path.
Psalm 119:105

This Book of the Law shall not depart
from your mouth, but you shall meditate in it day and
night, that you may observe to do according to all that is
written in it. For then you will make your way
prosperous, and then you will have good success.
Joshua 1:8

Dearest One,

Remain faithful to listening to Me in prayer. By listening to Me, your hearing will deepen and expand. It takes time in prayer to begin to hear Me. Keep making the love sacrifice of your time. You really have nothing morc important to do with your life and your day than to give time back to the One who gives time to you.

Believe that all I have said to you will come to pass. I am Truth, and no lie can be found upon My lips. Honor Me with your belief and your trust. It is easy to trust for those things which matter little to you, but to trust in those matters where your heart deeply desires is a different matter. Trust where you desire the most in your life, and see what I will do.

Life is about what I proclaim in My Word. The mindset of the world confuses My messages to My people. All that you need is revelation from My Spirit, and My Word will be opened unto you. Do not give up prematurely. Stop avoiding My Word, and stop using it sparingly, as though a little bit can sustain you. My Word is sustenance and life. Do not ration My Word. Use it amply, and you will see ample results in your life. If you want to grow, this is what you must do to mature. Baby amounts of Scripture are for baby Christians. Larger amounts of Scripture are for the fully mature, who can digest more. You will never be able to read too much, but you are able to read too little, and then you will grow spiritually weaker.

Read Scripture according to where you are, and do not fool yourself. My Word is not distasteful and bitter, but sweet to the taste, as honey is to the lips. Taste and see. You will develop a taste for My Word if you are faithful to the tasting.

Day 106: Spend Time with the Lord

Come to Me, all you who labor and are heavy laden, and I will give you rest. Take My yoke upon you and learn from Me, for I am gentle and lowly in heart, and you will find rest for your souls.
For My yoke is easy and My burden is light.
Matthew 11:28-30

Abide in me, and I in you. As the branch cannot bear fruit by itself, unless it abides in the vine, neither can you, unless you abide in me. I am the vine; you are the branches. Whoever abides in me and I in him, he it is that bears much fruit, for apart from me you can do nothing.
John 15:4-5 ESV

Dearest Child,

Rest in Me when you are weary. Simply come and lean into Me. You cannot give what you do not have, but you can give Me your will by simply coming to Me just as you are.

Come, and I will renew you. Come and be filled. I desire to love you and to renew you. I am not disappointed by your pain or your lethargy. Simply call out to Me. I know exactly where you are. There is no need to apologize. Just give Me what you have, and it will be more than enough.

You will never come to Me and leave more exhausted. You need Me the most at these times. Do not turn your back because you are without strength. All it takes is a decision of your will. Lean into My heart of love. This is enough.

Day 107: Pay Attention to Your Thoughts

For though we walk in the flesh, we do not war according to the flesh. For the weapons of our warfare are not carnal but mighty in God for pulling down strongholds, casting down arguments and every high thing that exalts itself against the knowledge of God, bringing every thought into captivity to the obedience of Christ, and being ready to punish all disobedience when your obedience is fulfilled.
2 Corinthians 10:3-6

If then you were raised with Christ, seek those things which are above, where Christ is, sitting at the right hand of God. Set your mind on things above, not on things on the earth.
Colossians 3:1-2

Beloved One,

You must fight the battle of your thought life. The discourager always wants to destroy your joy. He sows seeds of doubt whenever you entertain his thoughts as yours. Be alert to the ploys of the enemy. He gets you to question what you know. "Did God really say this?" or, "Who am I to receive this from God?" Instead of entertaining doubts, question their source. Who would want you to believe this statement? When doubts become at home in your mind, they can become rooted in your beliefs.

Do daily housekeeping. Which thoughts and beliefs need to be saved, and which need to be thrown away? Just because the thoughts are not familiar, does not mean that they originated as yours. You must use a better inner radar to detect oncoming thoughts that are destructive. Do not allow low-flying thought attacks from the enemy to come in under your radar. Question your thoughts. Be alert and not complacent.

I do speak to My children. This is normal. What is also normal is that the enemy is always speaking into the atmosphere. Do not be taken prisoner by the thoughts of the enemy. Familiar thoughts, unquestioned, become beliefs. You need to regain lost inner territory. Who would benefit from this belief? Recognize the tactics of the dark one. The dark thoughts take you to dark places. I am the Light of the World. There is freedom in truth. Be liberated from the tormenting thoughts of doubt.

Choose this day life and not death. I have given you discernment. You are free. Do not put yourself in a prison of doubt. You already know who the author of that is. Go down a different road. Questioning truth is a trap. Do not take this bait.

Day 108: Press Toward the Goal

Not that I have already attained, or am already perfected; but I press on, that I may lay hold of that for which Christ Jesus has also laid hold of me. Brethren, I do not count myself to have apprehended; but one thing I do, forgetting those things which are behind and reaching forward to those things which are ahead, I press toward the goal for the prize of the upward call of God in Christ Jesus.
Philippians 3:12-14

And do not be conformed to this world, but be transformed by the renewing of your mind, that you may prove what is that good and acceptable and perfect will of God.
Romans 12:2

Therefore we also, since we are surrounded by so great a cloud of witnesses, let us lay aside every weight, and the sin which so easily ensnares us, and let us run with endurance the race that is set before us...
Hebrews 12:1

Dearest,

Arise from your slumber. It is time to move forward in the Spirit. Be passive no longer. Move toward the goal. Pursue Me with your love. Do you hear Me calling you to be more active in your faith walk? I am not beyond your reach. Pursue Me with desire, for I do not want a lukewarm Bride.

Day 109: Put Aside Childish Beliefs

...that we should no longer be children, tossed to and fro and carried about with every wind of doctrine, by the trickery of men, in the cunning craftiness of deceitful plotting, but, speaking the truth in love, may grow up in all things into Him who is the head—Christ—from whom the whole body, joined and knit together by what every joint supplies, according to the effective working by which every part does its share, causes growth of the body for the edifying of itself in love.
Ephesians 4:14-16

When I was a child, I spoke as a child, I understood as a child, I thought as a child; but when I became a man, I put away childish things.
1 Corinthians 13:11

For though by this time you ought to be teachers, you need someone to teach you again the first principles of the oracles of God; and you have come to need milk and not solid food. For everyone who partakes only of milk is unskilled in the word of righteousness, for he is a babe. But solid food belongs to those who are of full age, that is, those who by reason of use have their senses exercised to discern both good and evil.
Hebrews 5:12-14

Dearest Child of the Father,

I behold you in love. This is the day of the Lord. I am here with you. Your belief is that I am at a distance, as far away as space is from the earth. The little child in you still holds onto this lie. Will you give Me the lie of My distance to receive the truth of My presence?

I am with you in love. I am not scowling at you in disgust. I am One who is beyond your limiting beliefs of my goodness. I am a God who loves you. My plans for you will come to pass. You are not here to bide time until you die.

Grace has given you life. Enjoy life, as it is My gift to you. Do not keep apologizing for who you are not. Live who you are. Love the one I love. Be the you that I created. I am not ashamed of you. I grieve when you do not see who I see. Present yourself as one who is purposed by God. You did not "slip through"—you were intended.

Day 110: Put Away Childish Thinking

And have you completely forgotten this word of encouragement that addresses you as a father addresses his son? It says, "My son, do not make light of the Lord's discipline, And do not lose heart when he rebukes you, because the Lord disciplines the one he loves, and he chastens everyone he accepts as his son."

Endure hardship as discipline; God is treating you as his children. For what children are not disciplined by their father? If you are not disciplined—and everyone undergoes discipline—then you are not legitimate, not true sons and daughters at all.

Moreover, we have all had human fathers who disciplined us and we respected them for it. How much more should we submit to the Father of spirits and live! They disciplined us for a little while as they thought best; but God disciplines us for our good, in order that we may share in his holiness.

No discipline seems pleasant at the time, but painful. Later on, however, it produces a harvest of righteousness and peace for those who have been trained by it.
Hebrews 12:5-11

My sheep hear My voice, and I know them, and they follow Me.
John 10:27

My Child,

Believe that I am God and that I am good. I have been speaking to My people ever since the first man and woman.

It is time to put away childish beliefs of a God who is silent. Will you exchange the old beliefs and lies for truth? Where does your loyalty lie? Are you willing to hear truth and to embrace it? It is not too late to begin anew. Step into a new dimension of faith. Believe and expect. Trust in My goodness and in My presence. Look for Me and you will find Me. I am able to communicate with you. Expect to hear from Me, and you will hear from Me more often.

Day 111: Reach Out in His Name

The King will reply, "Truly I tell you, whatever you did for one of the least of these brothers and sisters of mine, you did for me."
Matthew 25:40 NIV

Let your light so shine before men, that they may see your good works and glorify your Father in heaven...
Matthew 5:16

Greater love has no one than this, than to lay down one's life for his friends.
John 15:13

Dearest,

Behold, the King of Glory is with you. When you visit the sick and pray for the infirmed, I am with you. Press beyond your fear of how you will do this. Just do what you can, and leave the results in My hands. Trust My mercy, which is great. Hope in My goodness when all looks bleak to you. My heart is near to those whose need is great.

I love you too much to allow you to give in to the voice of the critic within. Do not hold back on reaching out to others. You do not have to be perfect. Love covers much. It is better to reach out and to be turned down, than to hold back and miss the opportunity at hand. Compassion is My gift to you. Use it generously. People may say no to your request to pray for them, but later they will realize that I was passing by.

Begin a new season of availability to those around you. Do this in My name, as I will always be willing to bless My friends. You only fail if you do nothing. Each attempt to reach out to others gets easier to do the next time. This is a place of beginning for you.

Day 112: Reach Out to the Lost

So He spoke this parable to them, saying:
"What man of you, having a hundred sheep,
if he loses one of them, does not leave
the ninety-nine in the wilderness,
and go after the one which is lost until he finds it?
And when he has found it,
he lays it on his shoulders, rejoicing.
And when he comes home, he calls together his friends
and neighbors, saying to them,
'Rejoice with me, for I have found my sheep
which was lost!' I say to you that likewise there will be
more joy in heaven over one sinner who repents
than over ninety-nine just persons who need no
repentance."
Luke 15:3-7

For I was hungry, and you gave Me something to eat; I was thirsty, and you gave Me something to drink; I was a stranger, and you invited Me in; naked, and you clothed Me; I was sick, and you visited Me; I was in prison, and you came to Me.' Then the righteous will answer Him, 'Lord, when did we see You hungry, and feed You, or thirsty, and give You something to drink? And when did we see You a stranger, and invite You in, or naked, and clothe You? When did we see You sick, or in prison, and come to You?' The King will answer and say to them, 'Truly I say to you, to the extent that you did it to one of these brothers of Mine, even the least of them, you did it to Me.'
Matthew 25:35-40 NASB

I will make you as a light for the nations, that my salvation may reach to the end of the earth.
Isaiah 49:6b ESV

Dearest Beloved One,

I rejoice when you come to Me and rest in My presence. You choose wisely when you choose to rest in Me.

Receive the truth of My Word that I gave you. I have come to set you free from the bondages of shame and fear. Do not fear what man will say or do. Instead, fear that some will perish because of not believing in My name. Fear displeasing Me—not because I am an unfair taskmaster, but instead that you would stray from Me.

The world seeks to entice you. Do not be confused by the glitter of this world. Choose what matters most to Me. I desire souls to be saved. Reach out to those who are lost. Invite them into My kingdom. Fear not what they may say in response to you. Instead, fear that their souls would be lost. The harvest is ready. Do not neglect the work of the Kingdom. Seek the lost and the hurting. Go after them in My name. I want none to be lost. Do this out of love for Me. I am pleased with you.

Day 113: Remember

Remember, remember My people,
I have carved you in the palm of My hand.
Remember, remember My children,
I have saved you by the blood of the Lamb.
You are My chosen ones and I have called you.
May you never turn your backs on Me.
Reach out and love one another.
My love for you will not end.
Feed the poor and the starving.
My Word will fill many voids.
Cement the cracks in the broken hearts
with the Word of the sacrificed Lamb.
My love alone is sufficient,
so turn not your backs on Me.
Come, My Beloved and serve Me.
I will walk by your side.
My love will light your journey.
Be not afraid of the dark.
My promise is more than sufficient.
Step out in trust of the Lamb.
I am waiting, waiting My children, so follow...
Step out in the love of the Lamb.
Go out and serve one another.

Walk with Me hand in hand.
I am waiting for you, My Beloved.
Awaiting is My sacrificed Lamb.
Go out and feed all the hungry.
Minister to those in need.
I will never forsake you, for I have carved you,
carved you in the palm of My hand.
Remember, My love is everlasting.
Remember the blood of the Lamb.
I am waiting, waiting My children.
Begin the long journey with Me.
Reach out your hand to mine
and follow the blood of the Lamb.
I am waiting, waiting,
so turn not your hearts from Me.
Remember, remember, My children,
for you I gave up My Son.
Remember, remember, My children,
you, too, are My chosen one.

Day 114: Rest in His Love

He who has My commandments and keeps them, it is he who loves Me. And he who loves Me will be loved by My Father, and I will love him and manifest Myself to him." Judas (not Iscariot) said to Him, "Lord, how is it that You will manifest Yourself to us, and not to the world?" Jesus answered and said to him, "If anyone loves Me, he will keep My word; and My Father will love him, and We will come to him and make Our home with him. He who does not love Me does not keep My words; and the word which you hear is not Mine but the Father's who sent Me.

John 14:21-24

As the Father loved Me, I also have loved you; abide in My love. If you keep My commandments, you will abide in My love, just as I have kept My Father's commandments and abide in His love. These things I have spoken to you, that My joy may remain in you, and that your joy may be full. This is My commandment, that you love one another as I have loved you. Greater love has no one than this, than to lay down one's life for his friends. You are My friends if you do whatever I command you. No longer do I call you servants, for a servant does not know what his master is doing; but I have called you friends, for all things that I heard from My Father I have made known to you. You did not choose Me, but I chose you and appointed you that you should go and bear fruit, and that your fruit should remain, that whatever you ask the Father in My name He may give you. These things I command you, that you love one another.

John 15:9-17

If we confess our sins, He is faithful and just to forgive us our sins and to cleanse us from all unrighteousness.
1 John 1:9

Dear One,

Do you believe that My love for you is beyond measure? I have come that you would have freedom. I love you. Move into a new place of belonging. You belong to the kingdom of God, and in My kingdom there is freedom. Move in the freedom of being the Beloved of God. Meditate upon this, as it will empower you to move in a new way, My love.

You are not what you have done. You are who I say you are. Live in the freedom of being loved. You do not need to earn My love—you already have it. Be. Come from a place of being, not doing. Rest in the safety of being loved just as you are.

Day 115: Sacred Possession

For if you live according to the flesh you will die; but if by the Spirit you put to death the deeds of the body, you will live. For as many as are led by the Spirit of God, these are sons of God. For you did not receive the spirit of bondage again to fear, but you received the Spirit of adoption by whom we cry out, "Abba, Father." The Spirit Himself bears witness with our spirit that we are children of God, and if children, then heirs—heirs of God and joint heirs with Christ, if indeed we suffer with Him, that we may also be glorified together.
Romans 8:13-17

...in whom you also are being built together for a dwelling place of God in the Spirit...that Christ may dwell in your hearts through faith; that you, being rooted and grounded in love, may be able to comprehend with all the saints what is the width and length and depth and height—to know the love of Christ which passes knowledge; that you may be filled with all the fullness of God.
Ephesians 2:22, 3:17-19

Jesus answered and said to him, "If anyone loves Me, he will keep My word; and My Father will love him, and We will come to him and make Our home with him."
John 14:23

Dearest Beloved,

Behold, the King of Glory resides in your heart. Rejoice in the good news. You are inhabited by the very presence of God. Hear the good news. The King of Glory lives in His people, in a temple of flesh and bones.

Oh, holy Presence divine
Blessed is He among mankind
Oh, holy Truth
Oh, sacred Possession

Day 116: Seasons of Life

"While the earth remains,
Seedtime and harvest,
Cold and heat,
Winter and summer,
And day and night
Shall not cease."
Genesis 8:22

To everything there is a season,
A time for every purpose under heaven:
A time to be born,
And a time to die;
A time to plant,
And a time to pluck what is planted...
Ecclesiastes 3:1-2

Do not say,
"Why were the former days better than these?"
For you do not inquire wisely concerning this...
In the day of prosperity be joyful,
But in the day of adversity consider:
Surely God has appointed the one
as well as the other,
So that man can find out nothing
that will come after him.
Ecclesiastes 7:lo, 14

And He changes the times and the seasons;
He removes kings and raises up kings;
He gives wisdom to the wise
And knowledge to those who have understanding.
Daniel 2:21

Dearest One,

I call you My Beloved because you belong to Me. I am your Shepherd and you are My sheep. Seek pasture with your Shepherd. Do not seek what is out of your Shepherd's will. He knows what is best for you. Within the parameter of your pasture, you will find all that you need. Come in obedience with a willing spirit. Come and be tended. Look to Me for all you need. Be not anxious, but trust in Me and I will lead you safely home. Drink freely of My living waters. Cool yourself in My shade. Lean upon Me, and I will uphold you. Trust Me when I shear you. I know what is best.

What I give to you is for a season. Do not cling to it, as it is but a gift from Me. There are different seasons and different gifts. To each season there is need of a gift. Trust the Giver of the gift as well as the Giver of the season. I see what lies before you and I know what you need to grow. Allow Me to choose, as I am He who leads you. The sheep do not know more than their Shepherd does.

Day 117: Seek Him in Prayer

Seek the Lord while He may be found,
Call upon Him while He is near.
Isaiah 55:6

You shall hide them in the secret place
of Your presence
From the plots of man;
You shall keep them secretly in a pavilion
From the strife of tongues.
Psalm 31:20

Be silent in the presence of the Lord God;
For the day of the Lord is at hand,
For the Lord has prepared a sacrifice;
He has invited His guests.
Zephaniah 1:7

Dear One,

Sit in the throne room of your Beloved. This is not a time to ask for gifts for yourself, but to be a gift to the Son of Man. Empty yourself of all expectations and cares, and come boldly before the throne. To come before Me without anything is to be vulnerable and naked before Me. Can you trust Me this much—to come without speeches and rest in My presence? Come naked in Spirit, as you came naked into this world. Allow Me to be who I am, as I allow you to be who you are. Rest in My arms and abandon yourself to My love.

In times such as these, you will be changed on deeper levels than if you came full of so many things. This is not to say you should not come with your needs and burdens. I do ask you to come and lay them before Me. I ask for times of quiet with you in which you simply rest. Rest in quiet stillness, and I will take care of the rest. Take a step deeper into My throne room. Come and see where I live.

Day 118: Seek the Stillness

But we urge you, brethren, that you increase more and more; that you also aspire to lead a quiet life, to mind your own business, and to work with your own hands, as we commanded you, that you may walk properly toward those who are outside, and that you may lack nothing.
1 Thessalonians 4:10b-12

Draw near to God and He will draw near to you. Cleanse your hands, you sinners; and purify your hearts, you double-minded.
James 4:8

Truly my soul silently waits for God; From Him comes my salvation.
Psalm 62:1

Dearest,

In listening to My voice you will know peace. Quiet yourself, then listen for My small still voice. I wait to speak to My people. In stillness you will gather strength as you allow My words to feed you. Partake of the richness of My words. Savor My words, for they will bring health and life to you.

Do not run from quietness. Walk into it willingly. When you still your soul, you will meet Me there. Dare to sculpt time apart from your busy or not-so-busy day. Partake of what you were meant for: relationship with

Me. Befriend the stillness. Seek it and you will find a Friend. I am that Friend. I will not force you, but I will invite you to create a space for Me. I will honor your intentions.

Pursue My friendship with the dedication that you have given to other friendships, and you will discover One who will meet you there. I am your only forever Friend. In Me you will never be lonely. I will fulfill you, and I will never forsake you. You are My child, My delight. In silence I will restore you. Enter the rest, and rest in My presence.

Day 119: Seeking the Lord

For I know the thoughts that I think toward you, says the Lord, thoughts of peace and not of evil, to give you a future and a hope. Then you will call upon Me and go and pray to Me, and I will listen to you. And you will seek Me and find Me, when you search for Me with all your heart. I will be found by you, says the Lord...
Jeremiah 29:11-14a

But without faith it is impossible to please Him, for he who comes to God must believe that He is, and that He is a rewarder of those who diligently seek Him.
Hebrews 11:6

Dearest,

You do not need to worry about being lost, as you are not lost to Me. This place of feeling lost and disconnected is a familiar place to you. You do not need to feel My presence in order to be in My love. Keep doing what you are doing. In seeking Me, you will find Me.

It is not necessary to strive in order to be loved by Me. You do not earn My love, as I freely give it to you. Fix your eyes upon Me. I know that you are saying that you cannot fix your eyes on Me, as you are unable to see Me. Look through your spiritual eyes. Come to Me as you are, and that is enough for Me. Do not give up when you are frustrated. Trust more in Me than in your efforts to come closer to Me.

Day 120: Silence Is for Listening

Immediately Jesus made His disciples get into the boat and go before Him to the other side, while He sent the multitudes away. And when He had sent the multitudes away, He went up on the mountain by Himself to pray. Now when evening came, He was alone there.
Matthew 14:22-23

Be still, and know that I am God;
I will be exalted among the nations,
I will be exalted in the earth!
Psalm 46:10

Dearest Beloved,

I embrace your willingness to listen to Me. When you stop talking, I can start to speak. Silence is the open space where you pause to honor Me. It takes time to get through to My people because they are so busy talking. Silence is an invitation for Me to come closer to you. I am here and I love you.

Day 121: Spend Time with the Lord

If you then, being evil, know how to give
good gifts to your children,
how much more will your Father who is in heaven give
good things to those who ask Him!
Matthew 7:11

Every good gift and every perfect gift is from above, and
comes down from the Father of lights,
with whom there is no variation
or shadow of turning.
James 1:17

I am the true vine, and my Father is the vinedresser. Every branch in me that does not bear fruit he takes away, and every branch that does bear fruit he prunes, that it may bear more fruit. Already you are clean because of the word that I have spoken to you. Abide in me, and I in you. As the branch cannot bear fruit by itself, unless it abides in the vine, neither can you, unless you abide in me. I am the vine; you are the branches. Whoever abides in me and I in him, he it is that bears much fruit, for apart from me you can do nothing.
John 15:1-5 ESV

Dearest Child,

You forget that I know how hard it is for you at times. Turn your thoughts to Me and call out My name. This is all that I ask of you at these times. I do not expect the impossible, as I am a God of love. Neither be anxious nor despair, for I am with you in exhaustion, as I am with you in strength.

All is a gift from Me, and the gift I desire is the gift of your choice to turn to Me, however feeble it may seem. To desire Me is all that I ask of you. Choose the better portion. Choose the life that comes from following Me. Do not try to take any bigger strides to get ahead. I am in charge of your progress. I know the things that you wrestle with, and I know that you are weary of the battle.

Do not give up, and do not look back at the defeats. I am with you, encouraging you, and I will give you all the strength you need, whether or not you think it is enough. Trust My provision to you. I see the bigger picture. The path I have chosen for you is handpicked to draw you into being My special vessel. I do not make duplicates—only originals.

Day 122: Spend Your Time Wisely

Rest in the Lord, and wait patiently for Him...
Psalm 37:7

Let love be without hypocrisy. Abhor what is evil. Cling to what is good. Be kindly affectionate to one another with brotherly love, in honor giving preference to one another; not lagging in diligence, fervent in spirit, serving the Lord; rejoicing in hope, patient in tribulation, continuing steadfastly in prayer; distributing to the needs of the saints, given to hospitality.
Romans 12:9-13

See then that you walk circumspectly, not as fools but as wise, redeeming the time, because the days are evil.
Ephesians 5:15-16

Dearest Child,

This is a holy time and you are resting on holy ground. Whenever you come before Me to worship Me or wait upon Me, I am waiting for you. Honor this time, for it is holy. This time is more important than phone calls, television, or reading something worthwhile. This is the better portion, and this is where I call you to come and meet with Me.

Watch and wait upon Me. Write My words to you. Read My Word and be renewed, even when to do so is last upon your list of "want-to-dos." Give Me your "want-to-dos"—I will transform them. Choose from the Spirit and not from the flesh. Do not get spiritually malnourished by putting off what you know is best for you, only to choose that which is easiest for you to do. Take proper care of yourself, and use wisdom in how you use your time.

Do not be too busy for Me. Reach out and choose the better portion. Choose that which brings life, and not that which simply fills your life. Leisure is important, and I want you to have rest, but time with Me each day is essential. Remember to whom you belong. It is rude as well as foolish to neglect the most important part of your life. You will find life, which you have always wanted, available to you by making daily sacrificial offerings of time with Me. It requires effort to read My Word. Do so as a love gift to Me. Give this to Me, and I will give to you that which you seek: abundant life.

Do not worry about how, when, or if I will do this. I will do it. Simply do what I say, and leave the rest to Me. When you are doing what I say, you will not have time to be entertaining other thoughts, which do not bring life, but death. Come and enter into life in the Spirit.

Day 123: Spiritual Encouragement

All Scripture is given by inspiration of God, and is profitable for doctrine, for reproof, for correction, for instruction in righteousness, that the man of God may be complete, thoroughly equipped for every good work.
2 Timothy 3:16-17

But He answered and said, "It is written, 'Man shall not live by bread alone, but by every word that proceeds from the mouth of God.'"
Matthew 4:4

This Book of the Law shall not depart from your mouth, but you shall meditate in it day and night, that you may observe to do according to all that is written in it. For then you will make your way prosperous, and then you will have good success.
Joshua 1:8

My Child,

Do not give in to spiritual apathy. Fight back. Open the Word and read it. Come out of agreement that the Bible is too difficult to understand. Read it until it breaks open. Wake up your spirit by reading the Word. The Word of God will raise you to another level.

What feels like punishment to a child is spiritual warfare to an adult. No one wins except the enemy when we give up. Pick up the Sword of the Lord. The enemy quivers when you do so. Do not allow the enemy to take back the ground that has been won.

Day 124: Spiritual Growth

And so, from the day we heard, we have not ceased to pray for you, asking that you may be filled with the knowledge of his will in all spiritual wisdom and understanding, so as to walk in a manner worthy of the Lord, fully pleasing to him, bearing fruit in every good work and increasing in the knowledge of God.
Colossians 1:9-10 ESV

But, speaking the truth in love, may grow up in all things into Him who is the head—Christ—from whom the whole body, joined and knit together by what every joint supplies, according to the effective working by which every part does its share, causes growth of the body for the edifying of itself in love.
Ephesians 4:15-16

But also for this very reason, giving all diligence, add to your faith virtue, to virtue knowledge, to knowledge self-control, to self-control perseverance, to perseverance godliness, to godliness brotherly kindness, and to brotherly kindness love. For if these things are yours and abound, you will be neither barren nor unfruitful in the knowledge of our Lord Jesus Christ.
2 Peter 1:5-8

Dearest Child,

I am with you as you wait upon Me. I am enough to meet all of your needs. I am for you and not against you. I love to see you grow in strength. Turn to Me and I will minister to the deep places in need of My touch. You are not too difficult for Me, My dear one.

Rise up from the darkness. Rise up from the low places. Rise up as I call you to life in abundance. You can be more than a conqueror. You are victorious. Allow Me to use your pain for a place of growth. I will show you how to arise and walk in a new level of strength. Look at Me and not at your circumstances. When you look at your circumstances, you recoil, and when you look at Me, you get strength for the journey. You are not too wounded to heal. Nothing is beyond My reach. My child, I know what I have placed in you and I say, arise child of God, and be all that you can be in Me. Reach out to Me and I will help you. Make good choices. I am speaking—do you hear Me? I have spoken—take heed of My words. You are not a victim. Walk in strength. I will help you to stand, lest you falter. You do not have to be further along than you are. Just trust My timing. I will lead you and I will never drag you. I am your safe harbor. Rest in Me and be healed.

Day 125: The Dance of Life

Let My dance move through you. Let the dance begin. Shall we dance? Allow Me to lead you in the dance. I am your lead partner. I choose the rhythm. I call the moves by how I turn you and when I turn you. Sometimes I hold you close to Me, and other times I hold you at a distance from Me. I have never left you, but it can feel like it when you are "let go" to dance some steps alone. These are the times when I allow you to use what I have taught you, or when I want you to learn something new. You have gifts, and I call them forth by trusting you to move about in the anxiety of not being purposely led. I am there watching you move. I will not leave you alone at the dance, but I will allow you to struggle to learn. I will allow you to make mistakes. Wrong steps—mistakes—are not the end of the world. You learn, you adjust, you take new steps, and you eventually succeed. When you master that dance, I have another dance for you. My Father loves to watch you dance the dance of life. He is encouraging you. He is a proud Father who says, "That's My girl."

Do not be ashamed at your awkwardness in learning, as it is to be expected. Even one with good rhythm needs lessons in learning the proper steps.

Sometimes I allow different dance partners to dance with you. They each have their own style of dance. They each learned to dance from different instructors. I teach many ways. Each teacher has a different lesson. I am actively involved in waiting, while you learn from the others on your dance card.

I am the Master Choreographer. I arrange, I step in, and I direct. I suggest, I wait, and I watch. I am your partner, yet I allow you to have other partners in the dance of life. Hear the music; it is there. Sometimes it is a joyful tune, and sometimes it is a melancholy tune. Sometimes the music is soothing, and sometimes it is a frenzy of notes. I am aware of each note. It all fits together.

You need to be led, and you need to lead. You need to watch, and you need to initiate. Dance is passive and it is active. Dance is responsibility for your part, and not for what the other dancers do. You are accountable only for your part. You need to concentrate on what you are doing, and not be watching what others are doing. When you do so, you are ahead of yourself, and you miss the moment you are in. You may miss some of your steps by watching what is not your concern. I am the Choreographer, and it is My job to observe all of My dancers. Be My love. Get back into the dance. Do not be discouraged. It takes much effort to learn the dance, but it is so worth the lessons.

Day 126: The Favor of God

Thus says the Lord:
"In an acceptable time I have heard You,
And in the day of salvation I have helped You;
I will preserve You and give You
As a covenant to the people,
To restore the earth,
To cause them to inherit the desolate heritages..."
Isaiah 49:8

But let all those rejoice who put their trust in You;
Let them ever shout for joy, because You defend them;
Let those also who love Your name Be joyful in You. For
You, O Lord, will bless the righteous; With favor You
will surround him as with a shield.
Psalm 5:11-12

We then, as workers together with Him also plead with
you not to receive the grace of God in vain. For He says:
"In an acceptable time I have heard you,
And in the day of salvation I have helped you."
Behold, now is the accepted time;
behold, now is the day of salvation.
2 Corinthians 6:1-2

My Dearest,

Rejoice, oh favored one. I have given you much. Can you delight that you are favored by God? Do you realize that not everyone knows Me intimately? I give you My words of instruction. This is to personally guide you on your journey home. Can you believe the goodness of

Him who lives within you? I am involved in your life intimately. Will you receive such good news? I delight in you. I am a faithful Father who takes personal interest in His children.

Rise up, Beloved. Embrace the truth of your beauty to Me. I see you, My fair one. I long for time with you. Give Me the first fruits of your time, your best quality time. Resist the urge to procrastinate in spending our time together. The spirit is willing, but the flesh can be lazy. Tame the flesh by choosing wisely, before fatigue sets in.

Day 127: The Journey of Healing

You are my hiding place;
You shall preserve me from trouble;
You shall surround me with songs of deliverance.
Psalm 32:7

Though I walk in the midst of trouble,
You will revive me;
You will stretch out Your hand
Against the wrath of my enemies,
And Your right hand will save me.
Psalm 138:7

God is our refuge and strength,
A very present help in trouble.
Therefore we will not fear,
Even though the earth be removed,
And though the mountains
be carried into the midst of the sea;
Though its waters roar and be troubled,
Though the mountains shake with its swelling.
Psalm 46:1-3

Dear Child,

Forsake Me not, My child, for I have not forsaken you. The road before you is a rough one. Can you place your trust in Me? I will lead you and I will guide you. You have but to follow Me. Follow Me, oh My child, to places yet unknown.

The road within is rough; the road within has been unknown. Take My hand and walk beside Me, and you will never be alone. The road within leads to freedom. It is your promised land, your home—if you cross the desert, face the plagues, and keep moving on.

Do not turn and run for cover. There is no place to hide but Me. I am within and I am beside you. Please come and follow Me.

Follow Me and I will lead you down paths you once have known—known and then forgotten, because you felt alone. You are no longer alone. Come and hold My hand. I will lead you into freedom, if you can risk and go within. Within there is a darkness, a desolation and despair, but on the other side of those things is new life, if you but venture there. To follow Me is your choice. To follow is to trust. Can you trust your Savior? Can you forsake the rest?

The feelings and the signs are not for you right now. The desert is a lonely place. The desert is the cross. If you will follow as I lead you, I will lead you to new lands, new lands of pain and feelings, hidden deep within. These are but lands to pass through. They are not the end. I am your destination. I am the map within. I am your compass, if you listen as I take you on your way.

Journey, oh My child, to a new land for you this day. Take nothing but your faith and trust in Me.

Day 128: The Kingdom Within

Rejoice, oh most highly favored child. The Kingdom is within. Within you is a fortress of strength. Come to the inner city. Enter her gates. Come into the Kingdom of Within. Within is where I dwell, and within is where you will meet your true self. Within is a city that has much to offer you. It is a city to be explored and claimed; it is a city of light. There are many mansions within the city. Come and see what lies within. It is a city alone and as you go within, you will breathe the air of inner contentment. It is not bad to be alone. When you are alone, you are always with Me, the Eternal Presence of Love, your Father. I permeate your very being and of the inner city within. Wherever you go, there also shall I be.

When you go within, you will be in a foreign place called "home." Come home to your birthplace. Come home to that place from which you have wandered. Come home to within. Take time to walk down the silent streets and breathe in the air of My presence. Let Me lead you by roads never traveled. Let Me lead you home to Me. I will call you into relationship with Me. You shall be My child, and I shall be your God.

Come deeper into the city. Come deeper into My love. Do not fear the city within. Do not fear the language of love. Do not fear the Spirit of peace. Do not fear the paths of alone. Come into the quiet and wait. Wait and you shall hear Me speak. I shall give you ears to hear in the silence. The silence has a sound and voice of its own. Come into the unknown to seek Me. Seek your beloved Lord. Do not take anything with you. Come to Me only with love.

Come to the city within. Come back to the "Mirror of Truth." Discover what I reflect. Bask in the glory of God. Stand naked before Me in truth. Stand before Me in virgin beauty. Stand before Me, My vulnerable one. Let Me lead you. Come into the city of Truth. Behold your Creator.

Day 129: The Lord Has Plans for You

For I know the thoughts that I think toward you,
says the Lord, thoughts of peace and not of evil,
to give you a future and a hope.
Jeremiah 29:11

But as for me, I trust in You, O Lord;
I say, "You are my God."
My times are in Your hand;
Deliver me from the hand of my enemies,
And from those who persecute me.
Psalm 31:14-15

Trust in the Lord with all your heart,
And lean not on your own understanding;
In all your ways acknowledge Him,
And He shall direct your paths.
Proverbs 3:5-6

Dearest One,

You are My desire. I have plans for you. Today is a new day and you get another chance to write upon this day with your life. What message will you leave? Will your heart be turned toward Me? I have given you life. Will you give Me your life in return?

Day 130: The Lord is Faithful to You

All the paths of the Lord are mercy and truth,
To such as keep His covenant and His testimonies.
Psalm 25:10

For the Lord is good;
His mercy is everlasting,
And His truth endures to all generations.
Psalm 100:5

Be strong and of good courage,
do not fear nor be afraid of them;
for the Lord your God,
He is the One who goes with you.
He will not leave you nor forsake you.
Deuteronomy 31:8

Have I not commanded you?
Be strong and of good courage;
do not be afraid, nor be dismayed,
for the Lord your God
is with you wherever you go.
Joshua 1:9

Dearest Beloved,

"Dearest" is My endearment for you. This is your name, Beloved. You are My Dearest. Can you receive such tenderness? "Dearest" is My name I give to you out of our intimate relationship. "Dearest" expresses My tender love toward you. See how gentle I am. Am I safe for your heart to turn toward? Am I not your Beloved? Will you love Me in return? Respond to Me, My love. I love to receive your love for Me.

You fear that I will stop speaking to you. My love for you does not have an expiration date. I am responsive to My Bride, and I will always speak to you. I am not limited in My ways to speak to you. You may experience limitations in recognizing when I am speaking to you. Do not limit Me by your limiting preferences of how I can come to you. Be open and allow Me to bless you in new ways. Do not fear that what has been familiar will be lost to you. My will is to be heard. My desire is to bless you, not to complicate things for you. My will for you is always for your good. Relax, and be open to what I am doing today. Do not miss the blessings of today by clinging to the blessings of yesterday.

Day 131: The Lord is Jealous For You

You shall not make for yourself a carved image—any likeness of anything that is in heaven above,
or that is in the earth beneath,
or that is in the water under the earth;
you shall not bow down to them nor serve them.
For I, the Lord your God, am a jealous God,
visiting the iniquity of the fathers upon the children to the third and fourth generations of those who hate Me,
but showing mercy to thousands, to those who love Me and keep My commandments...
for you shall worship no other god,
for the Lord, whose name is Jealous,
is a jealous God...
Exodus 20:4-5, 34:14

For I am jealous for you with godly jealousy.
For I have betrothed you to one husband,
that I may present you as a chaste virgin to Christ.
2 Corinthians 11:2

Take heed to yourselves, lest you forget the covenant of the Lord your God which He made with you, and make for yourselves a carved image in the form of anything which the Lord your God has forbidden you. For the Lord your God is a consuming fire, a jealous God.
Deuteronomy 4:23-24

My Child,

I love you too much to allow you to turn to other people instead of Me, when I am here for you. All you have to do is to call out to Me, and I will hear you. My answer is given when you call upon Me. If you keep on calling upon others instead of Me, you will always need them. You will fail to develop an intimate relationship with Me—one where you come, and wait, and see what I will do, and who I am. You will see who I am and how I work for you, if you risk turning to Me in faith.

When you turn to Me first, instead of to others, you are walking on the waters of your life. You will never sink when you turn to Me first. I promise to be there for you, and not to turn My back on you. Risk walking. Do not step out with part of your foot and test the waters, thinking that this is sufficient.

Have no other gods before Me. I do give you others to love you, to encourage, and to uphold you, but they are not substitutes for Me. There is a difference. Bring your troubles to Me first and not last, and I will honor that move of faith on your part. Begin to move today, and wait and see how I will honor those who honor Me. I will not permit My children to keep turning to anything but the one true God first. Remember, turn first to the One who upholds you, and then to the body.

Day 132: The Lord Names You

But now, thus says the Lord, who created you, O Jacob,
And He who formed you, O Israel:
"Fear not, for I have redeemed you;
I have called you by your name; You are Mine."
Isaiah 43:1

Listen, O coastlands, to Me,
And take heed, you peoples from afar!
The Lord has called Me from the womb;
From the matrix of My mother
He has made mention of My name.
Isaiah 49:1

Your eyes saw my substance, being yet unformed.
And in Your book they all were written,
The days fashioned for me,
When as yet there were none of them.
Psalm 139:16

Dearest One,

I behold you in love. You are My beloved one. You sometimes think that you are a nobody. I say that you are My somebody. Because of your lack of spiritual experiences, you sometimes doubt that you know Me. Allow Me to be the One who says who you are, and where you are on the spiritual ladder of experience and growth. Do not judge by others' experiences. You are not left behind. This is a season of your growth. This is not a season of being benched. Be available, and see what I will do when you are available.

I am your Friend, and I will grow you. Show up. Be My love. Do not strive. Just be Mine.

Day 133: The Master Art Restorer

So I will restore to you the years
that the swarming locust has eaten,
The crawling locust,
The consuming locust,
And the chewing locust,
My great army which I sent among you.
You shall eat in plenty and be satisfied,
And praise the name of the Lord your God,
Who has dealt wondrously with you;
And My people shall never be put to shame."
Joel 2:25-26

Instead of your shame you shall have double honor,
And instead of confusion they shall rejoice in their portion. Therefore in their land they shall possess double; Everlasting joy shall be theirs.
Isaiah 61:7

For we walk by faith, not by sight.
2 Corinthians 5:7

My Beloved,

I am the Master Art Restorer. I recover masterpieces that have been lost, forgotten, and "painted over" by life's circumstances, the enemy, and your beliefs and responses to pain. The masterpiece of "you" may not have looked special to some in your life because of their own limitations in recognizing your true value, or their own. There are those whose vision is flawed due to their life experiences, which handicap their ability to see.

I am the Master Art Restorer, who comes and removes all the old "paint" and identity of the image on the canvas of "you" in order to reveal who you truly are in Christ. When I restore and heal your image, you will see what I have always known and seen. You are My reclaimed treasure. My child, you are My masterpiece. I restore your identity. You are a new creation.

Day 134: The Power of Forgiveness

For if you forgive men their trespasses, your heavenly Father will also forgive you. But if you do not forgive men their trespasses, neither will your Father forgive your trespasses.
Matthew 6:14-15

If we confess our sins, He is faithful and just to forgive us our sins and to cleanse us from all unrighteousness.
1 John 1:9

He who covers a transgression seeks love,
But he who repeats a matter separates friends.
Proverb 17:9

My Child,

Give Me your painful memories and I will heal them. I cannot give to a fist, but I can give to an open hand and an open heart. Release what has imprisoned you, so that you can be set free to be all that you can be. Make room for more by letting go of what did not happen in your life. I am more than able to make up for what was not in your life. I can heal those broken places and make them holy places of strength and grace. Say goodbye to the last painful memory. Allow it to die so that you can move forward. Do not stay stuck in that place. Say hello to what I have for you.

Day 135: The Refining of the Lord

I will bring the one-third through the fire,
Will refine them as silver is refined,
And test them as gold is tested.
They will call on My name, And I will answer them.
I will say, "This is My people";
And each one will say, "The Lord is my God."
Zechariah 13:9

He will sit as a refiner and a purifier of silver;
He will purify the sons of Levi, And purge them as gold and silver, That they may offer to the Lord An offering in righteousness.
Malachi 3:3

I will give you the treasures of darkness
And hidden riches of secret places,
That you may know that I, the Lord,
Who call you by your name,
Am the God of Israel.
Isaiah 45:3

My Beloved,

Rejoice, for you are Mine and I am yours. My heart beats with love for you. This is the day of the Lord. Can you listen to My voice, My beloved child? Will you respond to My love? I am faithful. Will you be faithful to Me?

Draw near to Me, as I draw near to you. Listen and observe. I am near if you have eyes to see. I come to encourage you and set you free. Do not go digging in the dirt of your life as if to find hidden diamonds. I will bring to you treasures hidden for you to find. Allow Me to unearth the treasures for you.

You do not need years of refining; you need the Refiner of your years. I am here to do what man cannot. Search for Me, and you will find Me. I am hiding in plain sight. I want to be found by those who have eyes of faith to see. You do not need to be like another. I have created you to be an original. Allow Me to plant you, and do not attempt to transplant yourself. What I have given to you is good. Seek the good and be content. You are growing when you can settle into My will. You are not left behind the crowd.

I know what is best for you. The artist chooses which brush to use. The canvas does not tell the artist what brush to use or what to paint. The canvas awaits the strokes of the artist in surrender to his will. Allow Me to choose the brush and the strokes that I will use. Your life is My masterpiece. I know what colors to use to accent My masterpiece. Surrender to My strokes.

Day 136: The Truth Sets You Free

Then Jesus said to those Jews who believed Him, "If you abide in My word, you are My disciples indeed. And you shall know the truth, and the truth shall make you free."
John 8:31-32

Stand fast therefore in the liberty by which Christ has made us free, and do not be entangled again with a yoke of bondage.
Galatians 5:1

Behold, You desire truth in the inward parts,
And in the hidden part You will make me to know wisdom.
Psalm 51:6

Dearest One,

You are included in My family. You belong, and you qualify for love and healing. I am able to work within the circumstances of your life. I am not limited. I am able to reach into the secret places and set you free from the chains of bondage. You are not who you were before. The pain and the lies you believed were leading you astray. What you needed was the truth. I am the Truth and I am the Life. I am more than you can imagine. Let Me introduce Myself to you.

I am Love. Do not exile yourself as Eve did. Hide in Me and not in shame. I am the Truth that sets you free.

I have come to liberate you from the chains that enslave you. I am the Liberator. You are free. Do not accept prison as your home. Your identity is in Me. I name you as Mine.

Walk in dignity. Dare to believe the truth. Break agreement with the lies of the enemy. Do not live in shame. Walk away from your previous existence. You are above and not beneath. Do not settle for scraps, when I give you a meal. Enter into the Kingdom of My Father. There are places to go where you have not been before. Keep looking at Me, and not at your sins. I call you a saint and a believer. Walk with your head held high. Do not be downcast anymore. You are My love.

Day 137: Treasure the Lord's Words

For where your treasure is,
there your heart will be also.
Luke 12:34

Do not lay up for yourselves treasures on earth,
where moth and rust destroy and where thieves break in
and steal...
Matthew 6:19

If you seek her as silver,
And search for her as for hidden treasures;
Then you will understand the fear of the Lord,
And find the knowledge of God.
Proverbs 2:4-5

Dearest One,

Gather My words to you as a bouquet of flowers. Breathe them into your spirit. See how I treasure you, My love. I delight in the fragrance of your presence. Delight yourself in Me. Am I not faithful to My Beloved? Be still and rest in Me.

Value what I value. Follow in My footsteps. Have I not walked this path for you to follow? Be assured of your position in My heart. I will not keep you guessing, as I am not fickle.

Day 138: Trust in the Lord's Plans For You

As for God, His way is perfect;
The word of the Lord is proven;
He is a shield to all who trust in Him.
2 Samuel 22:31

I will instruct you and teach you
in the way you should go;
I will guide you with My eye.
Psalm 32:8

It is better to trust in the Lord
Than to put confidence in man.
Psalm 118:8

Dearest Child,

Be open to what I have for you. I have had to pry open your hands to make them able to receive from Me. Your hands easily go back into a clenched fist. I will fill them, and I will use them. Take time with Me to know Me, and then you will be more willing to be open to what I have for you.

Do not fear and do not despair. You are not who you think you are. You are much more to Me and in Me.

Do not clench your fists tightly around what I have given you, for fear that it will be taken away. Relax and know that I take and I give, and I am in control. My control is not the control of the world that dominates, crushes, and owns. My control comes from My Lordship and love. I allow free will, and I move in ways that are mysterious to My people. But remember, I know the full picture. I see what you cannot see.

Do not fear and do not anxiously look around to see where you have been deprived. I have given you what you need. There will always be more. I am more, and I am more than enough to satisfy your every need. Fill yourself with time with Me, and I will loosen the resistance within you. When you really know Me, you will trust Me with your life, and the life of your loved ones.

Allow Me to place into your life those I have handpicked for you, and you for them. When it is time to move on to another step, let go and know that there is more. Believe in that, and believe in the One who gives you that which you need and want. That which you want may not come in the expected form. I give you what is best for you, and that is what you truly want, even if you do not know it at this moment.

Day 139: Turn Daily to the Lord

Seek the Lord and His strength;
Seek His face evermore!
1 Chronicles 16:11

Do you not know that those who run in a race all run, but one receives the prize? Run in such a way that you may obtain it. And everyone who competes for the prize is temperate in all things. Now they do it to obtain a perishable crown, but we for an imperishable crown. Therefore I run thus: not with uncertainty. Thus I fight: not as one who beats the air. But I discipline my body and bring it into subjection, lest, when I have preached to others, I myself should become disqualified.
1 Corinthians 9:24-27

Do not lie to one another, since you have put off the old man with his deeds, and have put on the new man who is renewed in knowledge according to the image of Him who created him,
Colossians 3:9-10

Dearest,

I do not call you servant, but I call you friend. You are a friend of God. Your name is written in the Lamb's Book of Life. You are included. You belong. No longer are you an orphan.

Bask in My light. Sit at My feet, dearest one. I will give you manna. Come daily and be fed. You need this manna to grow beyond where you currently are. Will you come to the feast prepared for you? Will you come and allow Me to transform you? Sit before Me in loving surrender. I am willing; are you?

Come to the living waters and drink freely. Choose wisely, and you will drink from the waters of freedom and growth. Where will you show up? I give you choices. The world can be intoxicating, yet what I offer is eternal. Come to Me. I will teach you. Come to the school of spiritual growth. Your lessons await you. Rest in Me. Be transformed through My life poured out to you. Feed on truth. You get to choose what to feed on. Come within. I am within.

Will you wait upon Me? I will give you a new heart. Show up for our divine appointment. Come and be transformed. I will wash you of the effects of the world. Your garments will be washed clean. Come to our meeting and rest in My glory. You do not need to see; you only need to believe, that you may see the things of the Kingdom. Show up for Me more than you show up for television. Can you make the transition? Do you want to receive more? You get to make that choice. I am your willing Teacher.

Day 140: Wait Upon the Lord

But those who wait on the Lord
Shall renew their strength;
They shall mount up with wings like eagles,
They shall run and not be weary,
They shall walk and not faint.
Isaiah 40:31

Wait on the Lord;
Be of good courage,
And He shall strengthen your heart;
Wait, I say, on the Lord!
Psalm 27:14

Lead me in Your truth and teach me,
For You are the God of my salvation;
On You I wait all the day.
Remember, O Lord,
Your tender mercies and Your lovingkindnesses,
For they are from of old.
Do not remember the sins of my youth, nor my transgressions;
According to Your mercy remember me,
For Your goodness' sake, O Lord.
Good and upright is the Lord;
Therefore He teaches sinners in the way.
The humble He guides in justice,
And the humble He teaches His way.
Psalm 25:5-9

Dearest One Who Waits,

Wait in faith and wait faithfully. Do not give up or be discouraged. I have never left you. Oh, how you desire signs and wonders. I have given you a thirst for more, My hungry and thirsty one. You hunger because there is still more feeding necessary. You thirst because your thirst has yet to be quenched. I am not keeping you in a prison unable to satisfy your needs and wants. I am drawing you nearer to My will for you.

I am the more that you long for. Keep searching, but not in vain. There is more. Do not grow discouraged or become bitter. Do not disdain what is before you. Pray as you can. I am not here to entertain you, but to be adored by you. Keep coming closer. You will experience more, but first you must experience faithfulness in how you can pray. I am not judging you. Do not judge yourself, or judge Me by what I am willing to allow you to experience in prayer. Seek Me first.

Day 141: Don't Grow Weary

All around us we observe a pregnant creation. The difficult times of pain throughout the world are simply birth pangs. But it's not only around us; it's within us. The Spirit of God is arousing us within. We're also feeling the birth pangs. These sterile and barren bodies of ours are yearning for full deliverance. That is why waiting does not diminish us, any more than waiting diminishes a pregnant mother. We are enlarged in the waiting. We, of course, don't see what is enlarging us. But the longer we wait, the larger we become, and the more joyful our expectancy.
Romans 8:22-25 MSG

Blessed is the man who listens to me,
Watching daily at my gates,
Waiting at the posts of my doors.
Proverbs 8:34

Dearest Beloved,

You wait for Me to pass by. You want more of Me. Your longing for My healing touch is one of need and of desire. Do not grow weary of waiting. Waiting is not apathy. Waiting is not being put on hold. Waiting for My touch is waiting upon My timing. Waiting is knowing that I will and am passing by. There is still hope in waiting upon the Lord. Do not grow weary of waiting for healing. The one who waits exhibits faith, and this pleases Me.

I know that the process of waiting discourages you. You are wondering if you will die waiting, and never see the fulfillment of your hopes and dreams. You feel different than others, and you believe that I see you the same way. You wonder if this is a handicap to receiving from Me all that you want to receive from Me.

You, My child, are unique. I want relationship with you. I know you intimately, and I see you. You are not invisible to Me. I value you and I want to use you. Receive your value from Me, My priceless one. I love you.

Day 142: Waiting on the Father's Timing

For the vision is yet for an appointed time;
But at the end it will speak, and it will not lie.
Though it tarries, wait for it; because it will surely come,
It will not tarry.
Habakkuk 2:3

For we are His workmanship,
created in Christ Jesus for good works,
which God prepared beforehand
that we should walk in them.
Ephesians 2:10

Let us therefore come boldly to the throne of grace, that we may obtain mercy and find grace to help in time of need.
Hebrews 4:16

Dearest One Who Waits,

I wait with you as you wait upon Me. My timing is flawless. Your timing comes from your perception of now. I see the past, the present, and the future. I will neither rush nor delay My perfect timing to please My beloved children, who hunger and thirst for a move of God now.

Can you trust your all-knowing Father? Can you wait as one who has not been deserted? Can you wait as one who has a wise, benevolent Father? I am looking out for you. Your timing depends upon My timing. Will you relinquish your timetable for My timetable? I am at work even in the nighttimes of your life. I see your heart, and I am loving. Being loving is doing what is best for your children, even if it means being misunderstood by them. I love you enough to hold your disappointments and grief. I see beyond these, and I look to the future.

Oh, how I love you. My heart is tender toward you. I am not an angry, withholding Father. I weep with My children, and I weep for My children. Come to Me, as I give you your daily bread. I am your manna. Do not pass Me by for a substitute. Break open the bread of your life with Me, and allow Me to feed you. When you feed upon Me, you will not hunger or thirst. My presence is available to you. Partake of the life that is offered to you. I will give you eternal life.

Come to Me, and be refreshed. I am the living waters. Drink from Me. Drink as much as you want. I like you to be greedy for more of Me.

Oh, how you please Me when you turn your heart toward Me. Live from your identity in Me. Live as one who is standing in the Kingdom. You are standing upon holy ground. Do not give it over to the enemy.

Day 143: Walking in the Spirit

I say then: Walk in the Spirit, and you shall not fulfill the lust of the flesh. For the flesh lusts against the Spirit, and the Spirit against the flesh; and these are contrary to one another, so that you do not do the things that you wish. But if you are led by the Spirit, you are not under the law. Now the works of the flesh are evident, which are: adultery, fornication, uncleanness, lewdness, idolatry, sorcery, hatred, contentions, jealousies, outbursts of wrath, selfish ambitions, dissensions, heresies, envy, murders, drunkenness, revelries, and the like; of which I tell you beforehand, just as I also told you in time past, that those who practice such things will not inherit the kingdom of God. But the fruit of the Spirit is love, joy, peace, longsuffering, kindness, goodness, faithfulness, gentleness, self-control. Against such there is no law. And those who are Christ's have crucified the flesh with its passions and desires. If we live in the Spirit, let us also walk in the Spirit. Let us not become conceited, provoking one another, envying one another.
Galatians 5:16-25

For you were once darkness, but now you are light in the Lord. Walk as children of light...
Ephesians 5:8

We are confident, yes, well pleased rather to be absent from the body and to be present with the Lord. Therefore we make it our aim, whether present or absent, to be well pleasing to Him. For we must all appear before the judgment seat of Christ, that each one may receive the things done in the body, according to what he has done, whether good or bad.
2 Corinthians 5:8-10

Dearest Beloved of the Father,

I remember you always. You are not forgotten. Neither are you forgettable. Do you realize the price of My love for you? My love for you cost Me My life. Your love for Me will cost you your life. Will you die to yourself and live for Me?

How much of the kingdom of God do you want to walk in? Will you exchange this world for My world? Your walk with Me will be on a different dimension when you turn fully to Me. Breathe in the peace of My presence with you. Beware of situations that keep you from love. Choose love frequently over worldly responses.

Day 144: You Are Being Healed

But may the God of all grace,
who called us to His eternal glory by Christ Jesus, after you have suffered a while, perfect, establish, strengthen, and settle you.
1 Peter 5:10

The Lord is near to those who have a broken heart,
And saves such as have a contrite spirit.
Psalm 34:18

Why are you cast down, O my soul?
And why are you disquieted within me?
Hope in God, for I shall yet praise Him
For the help of His countenance.
Psalm 42:5

Dearest Beloved One,

Let hope arise. Your wounding does not keep Me away from you. I do not grow discouraged as you do when you have challenges. You are being refined in the furnace of love. Do not be discouraged. I am not surprised at what is rising to the surface. Can you trust Me with the raw pain that is oozing to the surface?

Fear not. I am with you. You have not disappointed Me with your responses. Remember who I am. I am He who knows you better than you know yourself.

Your time is coming to be the person of God that I see in you. Do not be ashamed. Lift up your head and look into My eyes of love. I am with you always.

Day 145: You Are God's Treasure

For you are a people holy to the Lord your God. The Lord your God has chosen you out of all the peoples on the face of the earth to be his people, his treasured possession.
Deuteronomy 7:6 NIV

For you are a holy people to the Lord your God, and the Lord has chosen you to be a people for Himself, a special treasure above all the peoples who are on the face of the earth.
Deuteronomy 14:2

And they shall call them The Holy People,
The Redeemed of the Lord;
And you shall be called Sought Out,
A City Not Forsaken.
Isaiah 62:12

Beloved,

Hear Me speak to you a message of value. You are My treasure. I paid the price for you with My very own blood. You were ransomed to darkness and death. I could not forget you. I know who you are. The enemy can only deceive and confuse. I bring clarity and life. My love for you, My Beloved, is beyond measure. I paid the price in full. Your freedom has been won. No longer walk as a prisoner. You are set free.

You are a child of God, and no one gets to say anything to the contrary. Hold your head up and gaze into the eyes of your Redeemer. You are free. You are free. You are free. Do not put yourself back into captivity by your beliefs. Give Me the lies of the enemy. Trust in Me, as I am trustworthy. Bride of Christ, rise up. Stand before Me in courage. You are My Beloved. No more will you walk in shame. You have dignity, My valuable one. Step out in the truth of your value. You matter in the Kingdom. There is a purpose for you. You are significant. Value has been placed upon you. You are mine, and I am yours.

Day 146: You Are His Child

Let your light so shine before men, that they may see your good works and glorify your Father in heaven...
Matthew 5:16

For you did not receive the spirit of bondage again to fear, but you received the Spirit of adoption by whom we cry out, "Abba, Father." The Spirit Himself bears witness with our spirit that we are children of God...
Romans 8:15-16

But when the fullness of the time had come, God sent forth His Son, born of a woman, born under the law, to redeem those who were under the law, that we might receive the adoption as sons. And because you are sons, God has sent forth the Spirit of His Son into your hearts, crying out, "Abba, Father!"
Galatians 4:4-7

Dearest Child of the King,

Rise up. You were created to bring glory to the King. Step out of the shadows, My fair one. Cast your own shadow. Today is a new day. Reflect your Maker's glory.

Delight yourself in Me, My love, as I delight Myself in you. Sing songs of gratitude over Me. Gratefulness is a prayer offered to Me. Remember He who gives you all things. Train yourself to see My handprints upon your life. I appreciate appreciation. With a heart full of gratefulness, you will experience joy. In the joy of the Lord is your strength. You are stronger than you realize. I am stretching your borders. Lean into Me, as I direct your path.

Day 147: You Are His Temple

Or do you not know that your body
is the temple of the Holy Spirit
who is in you, whom you have from God,
and you are not your own?
For you were bought at a price;
therefore glorify God in your body
and in your spirit, which are God's.
1 Corinthians 6:19-20

Do you not know that you are the temple of God
and that the Spirit of God dwells in you?
If anyone defiles the temple of God,
God will destroy him.
For the temple of God is holy,
which temple you are.
1 Corinthians 3:16-17

And what agreement has the temple of God with idols?
For you are the temple of the living God.
As God has said: "I will dwell in them and walk among
them. I will be their God,
and they shall be My people."
2 Corinthians 6:16

My Fair One,

I rejoice to be your Shepherd. You are My little lamb, and I will protect you from the wolves that would devour you—the wolves within and without. The part of you that destroys your self-worth is like a wolf that captures an innocent lamb and devours it. There is a part of you that pounces upon and chews on another part of yourself. You pounce on, attack, and chew up the weak part of yourself, instead of being gentle, loving, and tender with the weaker part of your being.

Do not lay in wait for that weaker part to be less than perfect, and then betray it, like Judas betrayed Me. He betrayed Me with a kiss. How many times do you betray yourself? How often do you betray yourself by denying the good within?

I want you to see the good within you, the weak part of yourself—to see all of yourself, and not destroy yourself. Do not destroy My temple. When you start to take the foundation apart, brick by brick, in a forceful nature, you are destroying the temple that is you. When sections of wall are missing, the building cannot stand. When you repeatedly tear down parts of yourself, it is more difficult for you to stand, to save face, and to be strong.

Hope in Me. Look to Me to see your image. Look to Me for strength, protection, and guidance. Do not destroy My temple by writing ugly words about yourself on its walls. I dwell within. Do not tear down My temple by eating too much, sleeping too little, and by making disparaging remarks about yourself.

Fill yourself with good words, good food, exercise, and time with Me. Do not destroy the place where I dwell. It can be a royal palace, or it can be a wreck of a house. I am still within, but you maintain it. You are the keeper of the grounds. You are the interior decorator. You furnish the music, and you provide the atmosphere.

Do you bring peace or chaos into your temple? Do you pollute the air with negative words, or do you keep your thoughts, your hope, and your trust in Me? Do you know the treasure that lies within? How do you choose to contain the treasure that I have given you? Do you polish the container and keep it as beautiful as it can be, or do you let it get run down and look sloppy? Do you cherish and take care of the only container that you have for the Bread of Life, or do you desecrate the temple by lack of reverence for what lies within?

Be gentle, for you are holy, precious, and special. I live within. I am wed to you. Are you ready for your Bridegroom, or are you running around unprepared, thinking you will get things together one day or the next? The time is now. Be the best that you can be for today, all for love of Me.

Day 148: You Are Pardoned of Your Sins

Blessed is he whose transgression is forgiven,
Whose sin is covered.
Blessed is the man to whom the Lord does not impute iniquity,
And in whose spirit there is no deceit.
Psalm 32:1-2

He will again have compassion on us,
And will subdue our iniquities.
You will cast all our sins
Into the depths of the sea.
Micah 7:19

I, even I, am He who blots out your transgressions for My own sake;
And I will not remember your sins.
Isaiah 43:25

My Child,

I believe in you. Believe in what I speak to you. You think that it is too good to be true that the Lord would speak to the likes of you. I came and I died for the "likes of you." Do not waste what has been poured into your life due to your own poor self-worth. If you were without worth, I never would have come for you. Will you believe Me? Can you trust My love for you? Am I not the Truth? Can I lie? You do not know how to receive such a great gift because of how you see yourself.

You are My Beloved. Embrace what is difficult, and let go of the lies about who you are. You have tunnel vision in regards to who you are. Your focus is upon your failings. I see more than your failings; I see the entire picture. Your history did not end in the past. Move beyond the faults to the truth. My child, you have been in a self-imposed exile. You have been in a prison that I did not make. I have paroled you. I have come to set the captives free. I have come to heal the hearts of the brokenhearted. Be merciful to My Beloved. Set her free, that she may live and not just "do time." You are released and the door is open. This is the good news. Your sins have been nailed to the cross. Rejoice—I never expected perfection from you.

Do not hide in a prison of shame. You are not alone, and you are not the greatest of sinners. Pardon yourself, as you are pardoned. Quit living in barracks that were liberated. You are free. Change is possible.

Day 149: You Are Seated in Heavenly Places

But God, who is rich in mercy, because of His great love with which He loved us, even when we were dead in trespasses, made us alive together with Christ (by grace you have been saved), and raised us up together, and made us sit together in the heavenly places in Christ Jesus...
Ephesians 2:4-6

Blessed be the God and Father of our Lord Jesus Christ, who has blessed us with every spiritual blessing in the heavenly places in Christ...
that the God of our Lord Jesus Christ,
the Father of glory, may give to you the spirit of wisdom and revelation in the knowledge of Him,
the eyes of your understanding being enlightened; that you may know what is the hope of His calling, what are the riches of the glory of His inheritance in the saints, and what is the exceeding greatness of His power toward us who believe, according to the working of His mighty power which He worked in Christ when He raised Him from the dead and seated Him at His right hand in the heavenly places, far above all principality and power and might and dominion, and every name that is named, not only in this age but also in that which is to come.
Ephesians 1:3, 17-21

But know that the Lord has set apart for Himself him who is godly;
The Lord will hear when I call to Him.
Psalm 4:3

Dearest Beloved of the Father,

This is a day of revelation. You are in the company of the angels of God. The Lord is with you. My Spirit inhabits you. You live in the throne room of the royalty of God. Be still and know that I am God. I inhabit the praises of My people. You are never alone. Walk in truth. Do not walk in the flesh, but in the Spirit. The flesh can deceive you by evidence that seems overwhelming. Look with new eyes. The New Jerusalem is at hand. Change your focus to one that is lined up to My Word.

Rise up to a new level of faith. What I have permitted will take you to new levels, if you will but use it as a stepping stone and not as a stumbling block. I am Lord and I see beyond all things to My purpose. Will you trust My will and purpose? Can I know what is best? Does the Creator not know the purpose of the created? Will you feel safe in the hands of the One who made you for His intentions? Submit to My will, which is good. You will know peace when you are in My will.

Day 150: You Are the Bride

"Let us be glad and rejoice and give Him glory, for the marriage of the Lamb has come, and His wife has made herself ready." And to her it was granted to be arrayed in fine linen, clean and bright, for the fine linen is the righteous acts of the saints. Then he said to me, "Write: 'Blessed are those who are called to the marriage supper of the Lamb!'"
Revelation 19:7-9a

The Lord your God in your midst,
The Mighty One, will save;
He will rejoice over you with gladness,
He will quiet you with His love,
He will rejoice over you with singing.
Zephaniah 3:17

As you therefore have received Christ Jesus the Lord, so walk in Him, rooted and built up in Him and established in the faith, as you have been taught, abounding in it with thanksgiving.
Colossians 2:6-7

Therefore, since we are receiving a kingdom which cannot be shaken, let us have grace, by which we may serve God acceptably with reverence and godly fear. For our God is a consuming fire.
Hebrews 12:28-29

Dearest Bride of the King,

I love when you turn to Me, My Beloved. I have spoken, and you have received My words to you like a bouquet of flowers. They are My love to you, presented in a form that you can treasure. I love to be admired by you. Am I not generous in My expressions of love? Love comes naturally toward you. Do you know why My love toward you comes naturally? It is because you are the object of My affection, and I am Love. Love comes from knowing the One we love. Delight yourself in Me, as I delight Myself in you. We have walked together many miles on this journey. Relax in My presence and enjoy Me, as I indeed enjoy you.

I am your love, am I not? Relax in Me. Show Me your love as I freely show you My love. This is a day for gratitude, as you walk closely with Me. I am grateful for your time. Be grateful for My presence in you. Clothe yourself in pleasing qualities. You, too, are My bouquet.

Day 151: You Are a New Creation

Behold, you are fair, my love!
Behold, you are fair!
You have dove's eyes.
Song of Solomon 1:15

...that He might present her to Himself a glorious church, not having spot or wrinkle or any such thing, but that she should be holy and without blemish.
Ephesians 5:27

Then I, John, saw the holy city, New Jerusalem, coming down out of heaven from God, prepared as a bride adorned for her husband.
Revelation 21:2

Dearest Beloved One,

You are the one I love. You are the object of My affection. Receive the good news that I speak to you this day. You are not forgotten, but remembered. I see you. Do not hide as one who is invisible. You are seen and you matter to Me. Rise up, beloved one. Stand in the fullness of your identity as My chosen one. Do not cast away your identity in Me.

A price was paid for you to be who I say that you are, beloved one. Hear those words said in love and truth. Do not see yourself as one who is invisible. There is a space for you. Step into it. Claim what is yours by your inheritance. Do not allow what you believe to exempt what I tell you. I am Truth and I cannot lie.

You are clothed in righteousness. Stop clothing yourself in rags of shame, which discount your true value. Dare to believe the truth. Walk as one who is loved eternally, and stop walking as one who is forsaken and without value. Do you not see that when you take on another identity than that which I have given you, you are in agreement with the enemy, and you are putting on his lie. Be faithful to the One who is faithful and true. Come to the altar of agreement. Put to death that which is a lie. Offer that as a sacrifice to Me. Be willing to put on the truth. Walk away from the altar a new creation. Retire the old worn-out wineskins; they no longer fit you, and they were never yours to begin with.

Clothe yourself as the bride that I have chosen. Do not put on the rags of the enemy, but instead clothe yourself in truth and righteousness. Walk in the integrity of your true identity.

Be seen and not hidden. I do not call you to live in the shadows, but instead, to live in the light. Cast your own shadow. Do not live afraid. I have only gifts of life for you. Live in fullness. I give you permission to be fully you.

I have not given you a mute button to conceal your voice. Do not mute yourself so that you can hide your identity. I have called you to be alive and not on hold. Do not put yourself on pause because of fear. Step out in courage, as I am with you. Step out in love. You are not less than others, and you never were less than others. It is time to come out of hiding and to move forward. Allow Me to take you with Me where I will go. I had no intention of keeping you a secret.

Be seen. Be. I am with you. Have no fear. You are not alone. I will take you gently into new places, as I realize that you need time to adapt to change. No more hiding.

Ready. Set. Go forth in My love.

Day 152: He Is Coming for You

Then the kingdom of heaven shall be likened to ten virgins who took there lamps and went out to meet the bridegroom. Now five of them were wise, and five were foolish. Those who were foolish took their lamps and took no oil with them, but the wise took oil in their vessels with their lamps. But while the bridegroom was delayed, they all slumbered and slept. And at midnight a cry was heard: "Behold, the bridegroom is coming; go out to meet him!" Then all those virgins arose and trimmed their lamps. And the foolish said to the wise, "Give us some of your oil, for our lamps are going out'" But the wise answered, saying, "No, lest there should not be enough for us and you; but go rather to those who sell, and buy for yourselves" And while they went to buy, the bridegroom came, and those who were ready went in with him to the wedding; and the door was shut. Afterward the other virgins came also, saying, "Lord, Lord, open to us!" But he answered and said, "Assuredly, I say to you, I do not know you." Watch therefore, for you know neither the day nor the hour in which the Son of Man is coming.
Matthew 25:1-13

Dear Bride of My Chambers,

Arise, My Bride, My young-in-spirit Bride. Arise and get ready for your Groom. Enhance your virgin beauty with loving thoughts of Me. I want you to ponder and eagerly await My arrival. Longingly await the One who comes. Wait with eager anticipation for the One who beckons you to arise and prepare yourself. For indeed, I am coming, and indeed, you have been called.

I am He who called you since I first named you. I delight in your thoughts of Me. Do not grow weary of waiting, and forget the One who calls you. Get ready, My Bride. Be alert and be prepared, for I am calling to you to come with Me to a place of deeper union. You must be faithful and not look for other idols. You need not grow weary of waiting. Use this time wisely; use it to be pleasing to Me.

Look and listen, for I am near. Can you hear My footsteps approaching? I have placed a hunger in you. Do not confuse this hunger for a hunger to be satisfied by things of this world. Only I can satisfy My hungry Bride. None other than the Bridegroom will satisfy the longings of your heart. Can you wait upon Me, My lovely one? Can you trust Me to not betray you? Would I deceive the one that I love? Could I be so cruel?

Day 153: Desire the Bridegroom

For your Maker is your husband,
The Lord of hosts is His name;
And your Redeemer is the Holy One of Israel;
He is called the God of the whole earth.
Isaiah 54:5

You shall also be a crown of glory
In the hand of the Lord,
And a royal diadem
In the hand of your God.
You shall no longer be termed Forsaken,
Nor shall your land any more be termed Desolate;
But you shall be called Hephzibah,
and your land Beulah;
For the Lord delights in you,
And your land shall be married.
For as a young man marries a virgin,
So shall your sons marry you;
And as the bridegroom rejoices over the bride,
So shall your God rejoice over you.
Isaiah 62:3-5

My Beloved,

Hear your Beloved, My Bride. Awaken, slumbering spirit. Arise—your Bridegroom is near. Keep coming. Keep listening, for I am nearby. I wait for you as you are waiting upon Me.

Be encouraged. Be of good cheer. Do not lose hope, for I am coming closer. I have never lost sight of you. My

Beloved, keep hungering for your Bridegroom. Press inward toward Me. I love to be desired. Stir the embers of your heart, that you do not grow cold. Blow gently upon the embers. Fan the flame of our love. Keep faithful to your journey, as I am faithful to you. Do not worry how you will grow, just trust in My promises to you. It is not too late for you, dear one. Keep looking at Me.

My timing is perfect, as are My plans for you. Grow in love for Me by remembering My love for you. Do not grow weary of waiting, for I am worth the wait. Do what you can to fuel the flame of our love. Be hungry without becoming bitter. Have expectant faith. I will not lead you astray. I am a gentleman.

Day 154: Give Your Heart

Then I heard what seemed to be the voice
of a great multitude,
like the roar of many waters
and like the sound of mighty peals of thunder,
crying out, "Hallelujah! For the Lord our God the Almighty reigns.
Let us rejoice and exult and give him the glory,
for the marriage of the Lamb has come,
and his Bride has made herself ready;
it was granted her to clothe herself with fine linen,
bright and pure"—
for the fine linen is the righteous deeds of the saints.
And the angel said to me, "Write this: Blessed are those who are invited to the marriage supper of the Lamb."
Revelation 19:6-9 ESV

Husbands, love your wives,
as Christ loved the church
and gave himself up for her,
that he might sanctify her,
having cleansed her
by the washing of water
with the word,
so that he might present the church
to himself in splendor,
without spot or wrinkle
or any such thing,
that she might be holy
and without blemish.
Ephesians 5:25-27 ESV

Dearest Bride of Mine,

I have been waiting for you in eager anticipation, for I knew that you would be longing for Me, as I long for you. Do you know what it is like to wait for you to make time for Me? Do you know how My heart yearns for you to come and sit with Me? I am not angry with you, but I could be if I did not love you so. I know the whys behind your resistance. You are not a surprise to Me, My dearest, as I know all there is to know about you, and I still call you My Bride.

Do not keep Me waiting upon you, as My patience can wear thin when I see you choosing others to give your best time to. If you knew Me as I know you, you would run to Me willingly. There would be no hesitation or resistance, only delight.

Our relationship will deepen as you make sacred our time together. Do not allow yourself to "run on empty," but fill up on that which is life-sustaining. I am the Giver of Life, and I will fulfill you. Other things may satisfy you, but I will fulfill you. Choose the better portion. Drink from the cup that I offer to you.

You are being trained to wait upon Me. It is difficult for you to wait, as you want to see the results of our time together. Each relationship is different. Do not compare our relationship to those I have with others, as I alone know the plans that I have for each of My brides.

Do not be jealous, as you are not forgotten or overlooked. I have plans for you that only you can fulfill by your yes. It doesn't matter how long you wait, but that you are ready when I call upon you.

Give Me your heart, as I have given you Mine. Do not give Me part of your heart and then withhold the other part of your heart. Give Me all of you, as I withhold nothing from you. Can you see what I have given to you? Will you be satisfied with the portion that I have chosen to be yours, or will you longingly desire that which I have given to another?

Can you see your gift? Will you embrace it in gratitude? Your experiences have formed you and they are valuable. Allow Me to dip into them, as I will indeed use them. Nothing shall I waste. The process is not finished, but it has indeed begun.

Do not grow weary of the waiting, as the process is important. I am grooming you, so do not squirm. Trust that I am capable, as well as loving. Come to Me and let Me finish what I have started. Say your yes to Me, as I have said My yes to you.

I love you more than you can imagine. I love you more than anyone ever has or will ever love you. Be Mine, My dear one. Be Mine.

Day 155: Arms of Love

Then one of the seven angels who had the seven bowls filled with the seven last plagues came to me and talked with me, saying, "Come, I will show you the bride, the Lamb's wife." And he carried me away in the Spirit to a great and high mountain, and showed me the great city, the holy Jerusalem, descending out of heaven from God, having the glory of God. Her light was like a most precious stone, like a jasper stone, clear as crystal.
Revelation 21:9-11

For I feel a divine jealousy for you, since I betrothed you to one husband, to present you as a pure virgin to Christ.
2 Corinthians 11:2 ESV

Dearest One Who Seeks Me,

Seek Me and you shall find Me. Desire Me, as I desire you, My Bride. I desire a passionate Bride to respond to Me. I desire your eagerness to be one with Me. Will you draw closer to Me? Do not be afraid of coming closer to your Bridegroom. I welcome you and I invite you into a dance of intimacy. Will you allow Me to lead you? Can you trust Me this much? Be yielded to My touch as I direct you on your path.

Settle in My arms of love. I will neither rush you nor hold you back from My will. My timing is just on time. Trust My purpose as I lead you. Do not fight the direction that I move you. I know the plans that I have for you, and I will move you in that direction. I am willing to change the tempo of your dance if you need to rest. I am a gentleman. I am in tune with you, My love. You are safe in My arms of love. Come closer to Me, and your life will change. I can never disappoint you. Allow Me to take you on a new adventure in our love. I will dance with you all the way home. Dance with Me, My love.

Day 156: Wait for His Instruction

I sleep, but my heart is awake;
It is the voice of my beloved!
He knocks, saying, "Open for me, my sister, my love,
My dove, my perfect one;
For my head is covered with dew,
My locks with the drops of the night."
Song of Solomon 5:2

Dearest Beloved,

Oh, My fair one, My dove, it pleases me that you want instruction on being a Bride. Being a Bride is a privilege. You have been chosen. You are spoken for, and that means that your heart belongs to Me. There will be others in your life, but the One to whom you are betrothed has first claim on your heart.

Set aside time to woo Me, as I, in turn, will want to woo you with my faithful love for you. Will you give Me your heart in a more intentional way than ever before? The Bride's heart is forever on her Beloved. Prepare yourself for time spent in adoration of your Beloved. Rest in the bliss of Love Himself. Be faithful to our times apart, as they will change your heart toward Me. The world will have less of a hold on you as you fully give your heart to Me. I am a jealous God and I desire much for My Son. Will you anoint yourself with oils of joy in coming into My presence? Do this in expectation. You know who you are meeting, so meet Me in desire and not in ritual. Do you want to be pleasing to Me or to the world? This is your choice. When you walk away from the world, the world has less of a hold on you. Be willing to do this. Choices change you. I do not ask you to leave the world, but to set yourself apart from the world. Who has your ear?

Allow Me to prepare you. I will teach you what you need to do. You do not need to guess. I will speak as you learn to listen. You do not need more than I give to you today. Remember the manna? Today is sufficient unto itself.

Day 157: Listen for His Voice

Set me as a seal upon your heart,
As a seal upon your arm;
For love is as strong as death,
Jealousy as cruel as the grave;
Its flames are flames of fire,
A most vehement flame.
Many waters cannot quench love,
Nor can the floods drown it.
If a man would give for love
All the wealth of his house,
It would be utterly despised.
Song of Solomon 8:6-7

Dearest,

Heart-to-heart is My language to communicate with you, My Bride. I have created you and I will never forget you. Lean into Me, and hear me speak to your heart. I am a tender God who draws you nearer to My Son.

Be prepared for intimacy by grooming yourself spiritually. Come into My presence in faith. Listen to My Word. Faithfulness is what I hold in high regard. I love to see you come to me faithfully, as I am faithful to you, My dear one.

You are making Me a valued part of your life, as you grow in wisdom of the spiritual life. I give you time and you return it to me. This is a sacrifice of love. You cannot outgive Me.

Enter into the Tabernacle of My Presence. You feel vulnerable because you do not see what I am doing. This journey is one of faith.

Day 158: Be Pure

I will greatly rejoice in the Lord,
My soul shall be joyful in my God;
For He has clothed me with the garments of salvation,
He has covered me with the robe of righteousness, As a bridegroom decks himself with ornaments, And as a bride adorns herself with her jewels.
Isaiah 61:10

Listen, O daughter, Consider and incline your ear;
Forget your own people also, and your father's house;
So the King will greatly desire your beauty;
Because He is your Lord, worship Him.
Psalm 45:10-11

Dearest Bride of Christ,

Rejoice in a new day, oh Jerusalem. The Bride has begun her preparation. Adorn yourself with purity, as a bride is pure. Do not accept the values of the world as yours. Take off what does not belong to you. I will adorn you as wholly Mine. Be alert to the wiles of the enemy. Separate that which is holy from that which is not. Exchange the old for the new. You are a new creation. I expect more from you, as I have given more to you. Do not settle for less.

Day 159: Carrying Yourself as the Bride

Therefore, my brethren, you also have become dead to the law through the body of Christ, that you may be married to another—to Him who was raised from the dead, that we should bear fruit to God.
Romans 7:4

Draw near to God and He will draw near to you. Cleanse your hands, you sinners; and purify your hearts, you double-minded.
James 4:8

...rather let it be the hidden person of the heart, with the incorruptible beauty of a gentle and quiet spirit, which is very precious in the sight of God.
1 Peter 3:4

My Dearest Bride,

You are important to Me and to My world. I have not forgotten you. You are set apart for My purposes. Remember My Words to you. Hold them in your heart, for they are truth and life. What I say will come to pass, for I am faithful, and I can do nothing against My nature.

When I call you My Bride, I hold you in high esteem and in a place of accountability. This accountability is not one to cause you stress, but to make you aware of the responsibilities of a deeper union with Me. I am not speaking from a place of law and performance, but of love and response to the One who calls you by name.

A bride awaits her beloved at the altar. She is ready and prepared for Him. The bride takes the time to prepare well in advance for her wedding. She spends time thinking of her groom, and he is the focus of her life.

Once there is a marriage, there is a responsibility to remain submissive to the groom. Pay attention to the words He speaks. Get to know your Beloved. Do not grow lazy, but stay alert; this is only the beginning. Be in the state of walking in the presence of the Groom and knowing who you are. Remind yourself of your position, and behave accordingly.

Walk regally, My Bride, for I am with you. Do not allow the world to influence you. My call is upon you, and you are capable of the call, and the name that I give to you. Clothe yourself in My righteousness. Await My timing with patience, not fear or disbelief. I know when you are ready for more.

Be with Me and do not squirm, but wait faithfully in love. I see what you do not see. Abide in Me, My lovely one. This time can be beautiful if you stay focused upon your Groom. Lean upon Me and learn from Me. I am your Teacher.

Day 160: Come as Yourself

O God, You are my God;
Early will I seek You;
My soul thirsts for You;
My flesh longs for You
In a dry and thirsty land
Where there is no water.
So I have looked for You in the sanctuary,
To see Your power and Your glory.
Because Your lovingkindness is better than life,
My lips shall praise You.
Thus I will bless You while I live;
I will lift up my hands in Your name.
My soul shall be satisfied
as with marrow and fatness,
And my mouth shall praise You with joyful lips.
When I remember You on my bed,
I meditate on You in the night watches.
Because You have been my help,
Therefore in the shadow of Your wings I will rejoice.
My soul follows close behind You;
Your right hand upholds me.
Psalm 63:1-8

Why are you cast down, O my soul?
And why are you disquieted within me?
Hope in God; For I shall yet praise Him,
The help of my countenance and my God.
Psalm 42:11

My Dear One,

Hear My love song to you. I am with you, My dear one. God is with you, My child of love. Can you hear those words sung to you in love? You are My dear one, and I delight in you. You are not forsaken, but beheld in love. You are not abandoned, but I stand beside you, believe in you, and hold you in My heart for all time. You are My child, My loved one. You have been called, and you are My chosen one. My child, I will not cast you away like a child who easily tires of a toy. No, I am with you for all time.

I knew who you were and who you would become. I did not doubt when I called you forth into being. I knew what I was doing, and who I wanted. I chose you, My child—you and you alone, just as you are. Come to Me as you are. Do not attempt to cover yourself to hide your identity like one covering his or her nakedness in shame. Come naked before Me. Come to Me, My Beloved. Stand naked before your Maker. Do not blush with shame, but open your arms and your heart to your Creator. I want to see your beauty and bask in it. Can you be vulnerable before Me? Will you sit in My presence without excuse, and simply be with your Bridegroom? I know you. You must be your true self with Me. Do not dress yourself in someone else's clothing, clothing you think is more appropriate attire for your Groom. Come to Me wearing your true identity and nothing else.

Let Me dress you as I will. I will choose that which fits you, and I will not attempt to make you into any other. I will draw you to Me with cords of love and enfold you. In love will you change and grow. You are beautiful in My sight, and I am not finished with you yet. Because I am not finished with you, do not come to the conclusion that you are bad. You are in a process of becoming more. I will adorn you with more, My Bride, at the appropriate times. For today, hear My love song wooing you to Me. Come to Me, My dear one, My Bride. You are loved, My dear. There is none to take your place.

Day 161: You Are Desired

Our soul waits for the Lord; He is our help and our shield. For our heart shall rejoice in Him, Because we have trusted in His holy name. Let Your mercy, O Lord, be upon us, Just as we hope in You.
Psalm 33:20-22

And not only that, but we also glory in tribulations, knowing that tribulation produces perseverance; and perseverance, character; and character, hope. Now hope does not disappoint, because the love of God has been poured out in our hearts by the Holy Spirit who was given to us.
Romans 5:3-4

Dearest Bride in Waiting,

Waiting is a process of hope and faith in the One who is calling you His betrothed. Wait as one who is desired by the Desirable One. You are not put on hold; you have not been benched. You are already chosen by the One who is Love. Beloved, you are Mine and I delight in you. I am refining you. Do not fear or be discouraged. Will you trust My timing? Allow Me to be in charge. I have not turned My back on you. I will never reject My chosen one. Hold fast. In due time I will raise you up. Keep faith in the Faithful One.

Day 162: Saying Yes

I still have many things to say to you, but you cannot bear them now. However, when He, the Spirit of truth, has come, He will guide you into all truth; for He will not speak on His own authority, but whatever He hears He will speak; and He will tell you things to come. He will glorify Me, for He will take of what is Mine and declare it to you.
John 16:12-14

My beloved is mine, and I am his.
He feeds his flock among the lilies.
Song of Solomon 2:16

Give ear to my words, O Lord,
Consider my meditation.
Give heed to the voice of my cry,
My King and my God,
For to You I will pray.
My voice You shall hear in the morning, O Lord;
In the morning I will direct it to You,
And I will look up.
Psalm 5:1-3

Dearest Bride of Christ,

I address you as My Bride. Does this frighten you, My dear one? Can it be other than this? I think not. You have given Me your vows. You profess to love Me, and you speak of a desire for more of Me. Do you not know that this is what intimacy is? Our love has been consummated by the indwelling of My Holy Spirit in your heart.

Our intimacy is deepened as you come closer toward Me. Can you lose yourself in Me? Can you abandon yourself in loving trust? Say yes, over and over, and you will be drawing closer to Me. There are many ways to profess your yes to Me. To life as it is, yes. To the immediate future, yes. To all that has been and all that will be, yes.

Does this sound too frightening to you? Can you follow Me blindly, saying yes, and know that I can change all things for you? Will you trust Me this much? Will you desire more of Me? Then come closer. Fear not, for it is I who leads you. Come, enter My chamber, My Bride. Do you still want to be with Me? Is this too close, or do you wish to wait? Come, My fair one. I invite you closer still. Where is your security? Look to the One who calls you.

Day 163: Keeping Your Vows

If you abide in Me, and My words abide in you, you will ask what you desire, and it shall be done for you...As the Father loved Me, I also have loved you; abide in My love.
John 15:7, 9

*...keep yourselves in the love of God,
looking for the mercy of our Lord Jesus Christ unto eternal life.*
Jude 1:21

*The eternal God is your refuge,
And underneath are the everlasting arms;
He will thrust out the enemy from before you,
And will say, 'Destroy!'*
Deuteronomy 33:27

Dear Bride of My Chambers,

My Bride, I am wed to you through My love and sacrifice for you. I have called you and chosen you to be My own. Do not take your vows to Me lightly. Vows are to be taken seriously. You are My Bride, and you must act like My Bride. Do not neglect your Groom. Anoint your body with time spent savoring My Word to you. Allow My Word to leave a fragrance upon your lips. Allow time spent in union with Me to grace your life.

Enter into My chambers as one who has been faithful to relationship with Me. I do not call you to do the impossible. What I am asking you to do is possible. Choose wisely and you will be wise. Choose love and you will have it to draw from. Make a bouquet of your time and present it to Me as a love offering. Lay this bouquet at My feet, My dear one. Next, enter in and sup with Me.

Day 164: Receiving His Vision

Therefore if anyone cleanses himself from the latter, he will be a vessel for honor, sanctified and useful for the Master, prepared for every good work.
2 Timothy 2:21 ESV

"Sanctify them by Your truth.
Your word is truth."
John 17:17

Grace and peace be multiplied to you in the knowledge of God and of Jesus our Lord, as His divine power has given to us all things that pertain to life and godliness, through the knowledge of Him who called us by glory and virtue, by which have been given to us exceedingly great and precious promises, that through these you may be partakers of the divine nature, having escaped the corruption that is in the world through lust.
2 Peter 1:2-4

My Dearest Bride,

I am forming you into the Bride of My choice. Can you sit still as I adorn you? Can you enjoy the process of becoming? Allow the oil of My Spirit to soften your heart in tenderness, as I prepare you for becoming one with Me. You are taken. I have spoken for you already. Will you come in to My presence and sit? Sitting is part of the waiting process, which produces qualities that are pleasing to Me. Waiting is putting down your agenda and surrendering to My plans for you.

Listen for My voice in eager anticipation as I cleanse your hearing from worldly influences. Allow Me to wash your vision of what it has seen in the world of the flesh. I will prepare you for another vision, which is seeing into the spirit realm.

Your ears will be fine-tuned for hearing My voice alone. Your mind will be renewed as you read My Word and you will be fine-tuned to think as I do. Do you see why the process of waiting to become a bride is lengthy?

The world will be fleshed out of you, while the Spirit will fill in those waiting, yielded places. My plans are good plans and they are worth waiting for. I do not make empty promises. I am good for what I say. You see, I cannot lie to you, My Beloved. Waiting upon Me is not being stood up. This type of waiting is pregnant with the promise of the future. These moments of yieldedness to Me, in which your will is dying to My will, are sacred.

Will you yield yourself to My timing and sovereign will? Can you trust in My good intentions towards you? I am the honorable One and I will not dishonor you, ever. The price of My love was costly. I am not a fickle God. I am unchangeable.

Day 165: The Dance of Intimacy

...but you shall hold fast to the Lord your God,
as you have done to this day.
Joshua 23:8

You shall walk after the Lord your God and fear Him, and keep His commandments and obey His voice; you shall serve Him and hold fast to Him.
Deuteronomy 13:4

My soul follows close behind You;
Your right hand upholds me.
Psalm 63:8

Dearest Bride of Christ,

Rest in My presence of peace. My peace is My present to you, My lovely one. I challenge you to come deeper into the quiet stillness. In quiet stillness, I am present. Rest in Me. I embrace you in love. Receive My love in a tangible form. I am your shelter. Seek Me, and you shall find Me.

Do not be shy, My Bride. I want you to pursue Me. I love being desired. Am I not the object of your affection?

Dance the dance of intimacy with Me. You are safe in My arms of love. Be yielded to My touch, as I move you in the dance of intimacy. Do not be fearful. Instead, be eager for My next move in the dance. I know where I am taking you. Be My Beloved, who is at rest in My arms. Will you trust My lead?

Come closer, My Bride. Show Me your heart as I move you in the direction of loving intimacy. Surrender to My will.

Day 166: You Belong to God's Family

But to all who did receive him, who believed in his name, he gave the right to become children of God...
John 1:12 ESV

See what kind of love the Father has given to us, that we should be called children of God; and so we are. The reason why the world does not know us is that it did not know him. Beloved, we are God's children now, and what we will be has not yet appeared...
1 John 3:1-2 ESV

...he saved us, not because of works done by us in righteousness, but according to his own mercy, by the washing of regeneration and renewal of the Holy Spirit...
Titus 3:5 ESV

Dearest Child,

You belong to the family of God. No longer are you an outsider. Search no more for approval and belonging, for what you seek is already available. You were chosen—chosen to be loved, regardless of what you said, did, or did not do. You cannot earn My approval. When you look into My eyes, you will always see delight, as I delight in My creation. That which you long for already exists. You are worthy of love and approval.

Do not allow another's pain or opinion to devastate you, as he or she is only one person, and what he or she says or does reflects upon his or her perception. Some people are limited in loving—that is their handicap. Do not define yourself according to another's limited perceptions of your behavior. Look at the bigger picture. Do not embrace the criticisms as truth when, indeed, the criticisms were a lie. Love expands; lies restrict. Do not step in and accept that which limits, names, and defines you when it does not come from truth and love.

Day 167: Walk by Faith, Not Feelings

For we walk by faith, not by sight.
2 Corinthians 5:7

For now we see in a mirror, dimly, but then face to face. Now I know in part, but then I shall know just as I also am known.
1 Corinthians 13:12

...while we do not look at the things which are seen, but at the things which are not seen. For the things which are seen are temporary, but the things which are not seen are eternal.
2 Corinthians 4:18

Dearest,

I delight in your times spent with Me. Your efforts to draw near to Me are pleasing to Me. I will draw near to those who draw near to Me.

Do not judge by your feelings as to whether or not you are making progress, and if I am near or far away. I am not the God of your childhood beliefs. I am as near as your very breath. If I were to withdraw from you, you would cease to exist, as My breath is breathing in you.

Believe the good news about My goodness. Believe that I want you more than you want Me. I am forming you even as you are struggling and feeling distant from Me.

Experiences are different from relationship. I am involved in the experiences, but experiences are not an intimate relationship with Me. Do you want a relationship more than experiences or healing? Only a relationship will satisfy your inner hunger and your deepest need. I am willing; are you?

Day 168: When Feeling Overwhelmed

Have you not known?
Have you not heard?
The everlasting God, the Lord,
The Creator of the ends of the earth,
Neither faints nor is weary.
His understanding is unsearchable.
Isaiah 40:28

Fear not, for I am with you;
Be not dismayed, for I am your God.
I will strengthen you,
Yes, I will help you,
I will uphold you with My righteous right hand.
Isaiah 41:10

The righteous cry out, and the Lord hears,
And delivers them out of all their troubles.
The Lord is near to those who have a broken heart,
And saves such as have a contrite spirit.
Many are the afflictions of the righteous,
But the Lord delivers him out of them all.
Psalm 34:17-19

Dearest,

Do not grow weary of the road before you. You only have to go one day's journey on it. Remember the manna in the desert—all that could be consumed was for that one day. I still give you that one day, which is today. Focus on this day. Stay in the day I have given to you.

Do not get ahead of yourself. You can only do one day's work in this day. Do not be overwhelmed by the days ahead. Position yourself in today. Choose accordingly. You do not have to be further ahead than you are.

Choose wisely. This is the day of the Lord. Enter into it prayerfully. Ask for help before you get behind. I know My will for you. I am willing to bring about My will in your life. Seek Me. I will help you.

Day 169: When Offenses Happen

Therefore I take pleasure in infirmities,
in reproaches, in needs, in persecutions,
in distresses, for Christ's sake.
For when I am weak, then I am strong.
2 Corinthians 12:10

If you were of the world,
the world would love its own.
Yet because you are not of the world,
but I chose you out of the world,
therefore the world hates you.
John 15:19

Moreover if your brother sins against you, go and tell him his fault between you and him alone. If he hears you, you have gained your brother. But if he will not hear, take with you one or two more, that "by the mouth of two or three witnesses every word may be established." And if he refuses to hear them, tell it to the church. But if he refuses even to hear the church, let him be to you like a heathen and a tax collector.
Matthew 18:15-17

Dearest One,

When you have been offended by another, shake off the bitterness and leave it with Me. Keep loving, and you will be like your Father. Do not give up. Keep moving forward. Do not get stuck in the quicksand of offense, as the enemy will sting you again and again while you are there. Move away from the offense to My love, which empowers you. Release and be free, or hold on and be stuck.

When you release what is difficult, you allow Me to come and change you. I am willing to do so much for those who want Me in their life. I am your loving Father. The one who torments you is the father of lies. To whom will you listen? I call you to keep moving past the offenses into My loving presence. I am the life-giver. The offender takes away from you. Step into what is available and away from the place of loss of connection.

I will listen to your hurts, and I will ask you to forgive and move beyond the offense to a place where what I say to you defines you, not the offense. Allow Me to define you. Do not give others the right to diminish what I have given to you. You, too, are not perfect, but you are being perfected. Do not crawl back into the quicksand of offense. This is not a place of life, but death. Come back to your Father and I will give you more. Keep reaching for the more, and leave behind the dead things that hold nothing good for you.

Choose life, not death. To which will you hold, and by which will you be defined? I give you a choice. Walk away with Me. I am beside you. I am your Teacher, and there is much for you to learn. Walk away and walk to

Me. Sit with Me, and you will find life. Sit with offenses and disappointments, and you will experience loss—life will be depleted in you. Choose life. I am Life. There will be pain and suffering in this life. Reach for Me to survive. I will help you. Keep reaching and moving with Me. I will help you move forward. I am your Father who moves with you. I was with you when all the moments of your life happened, and I will be with you for the rest of the moments of your life. Follow Me, and not the offenses and disappointments. I will not disappoint you.

Keep coming closer to Me. There is so much more to be revealed, and it is My good pleasure to reveal it to you. You can learn so much if you are open to love.

Learn and move on, My child. Do not move to a bitter place. Rest instead in love, as I am Love.

Day 170: When Others Dislike You

Repay no one evil for evil. Have regard for good things in the sight of all men. If it is possible, as much as depends on you, live peaceably with all men. Beloved, do not avenge yourselves, but rather give place to wrath; for it is written, "Vengeance is Mine, I will repay," says the Lord. Therefore, "If your enemy is hungry, feed him; if he is thirsty, give him a drink; for in so doing you will heap coals of fire on his head." Do not be overcome by evil, but overcome evil with good.
Romans 12:17-21

Make no friendship with an angry man,
And with a furious man do not go,
Lest you learn his ways
And set a snare for your soul.
Proverbs 22:24-25

Dearest,

Yes, I call you by name, as you are known by the Beloved. I call Myself the Beloved. Does this startle you, My love, to speak of Myself with tenderness? I am the Beloved of God, and so are you. You do not need to reach perfection before being named the Beloved of God. What I have done brings you into the throne room. Relationship is possible for you, and not just for a chosen few. There have been times in your history when you weren't chosen. My history changes everything.

Someone disliking you does not change your relationship with Me. I chose you and I will never "unchoose" you. You may turn your back on Me, or be too busy, but I will never not choose you. I know your flaws, and you are no surprise to Me. Nothing you will ever do will shock Me. I became disappointment so you would never have to.

Do not hide in the shadows of fear and shame. I know who you are and what you are capable of. There is good in you and I see you through eyes of love. I call you to serve, but not to be dominated by another. Do not be diminished by the diminishing words of others. Receive the truth to replace the lies. I will take care of your reputation.

Day 171: When You Are Afraid

This is my command—be strong and courageous! Do not be afraid or discouraged. For the Lord your God is with you wherever you go.
Joshua 1:9 NLT

Such love has no fear, because perfect love expels all fear. If we are afraid, it is for fear of punishment, and this shows that we have not fully experienced his perfect love.
1 John 4:18 NLT

They do not fear bad news;
they confidently trust the Lord to care for them.
Psalm 112:7 NLT

Dearest Beloved One,

I am yours for all eternity. You belong to Me. Is it too good to be true that I love you? Look through My eyes of love. I am not waiting to catch you in sin or pounce on you. I am not a threat; rather, I am on your side. I see the good you do. I know your heart's motives. I am never surprised, but I am moved by lovingkindness.

Exchange worn-out beliefs for new ones. I am on your side. I am rooting for you, as you are on My team. The enemy would have you believe that I am against you, as he is against you. Could I ever tire of you, who I created? I am tireless in My love toward you.

I am not insulted by your fears, as man might be. Man cannot understand you like I can. I alone know all your history. I died to redeem your history. Trust Me with your life. Your time is not yet finished. I am still at work. You may have many fears, but I am bigger than your fears. Give Me your fears, and I will dismantle them for you. Your fears are intimidating to you. I will stand with you against your fears. One by one, they will be dismantled. I will take you to a place of victory. You are coming out of fear and into love. Love has more power than fear.

I am fearless. Cling to Me as I take you to a new land of freedom. Hold onto Me—I have the keys in My hand. Believe that I am with you when you look fear in the face. Hold fast to Me and be at peace. I am your vindicator. Be yoked with Me, My love. Let us journey all the way home together. Dare to believe the Truth. I cannot lie.

Day 172: When You Hunger for More

The Lord is not slack concerning His promise, as some count slackness, but is longsuffering toward us, not willing that any should perish but that all should come to repentance.
2 Peter 3:9

My soul, wait silently for God alone,
For my expectation is from Him.
He only is my rock and my salvation;
He is my defense;
I shall not be moved.
In God is my salvation and my glory;
The rock of my strength,
And my refuge, is in God.
Trust in Him at all times, you people;
Pour out your heart before Him;
God is a refuge for us.
Psalm 62:5-8

Dear Hungry One,

I am here to feed you, My greedy, hungry one. You long for Me because I have placed a hunger for Me in you that will not be satisfied by any other than Myself. If you did not love Me, you would not want more. As I stretch your love for Me, you will want more of Me. Be satisfied with what you have by recalling My blessings to you.

You were created for Me, and you have natural longings to be noticed by your Maker. When you get disappointed and desire what others have received, you are a hurt bride, feeling ignored by her Lover. You long to be included and noticed by your Beloved. When you miss His glance or His touch, or even a word from Him, you experience abandonment and rejection of the One you seek to encounter in deepest union. You see others raptured in a loving embrace, and you sit on the sidelines and yearn for the same.

I do not torture or punish you. To do so would be cruel. Rather, I am drawing you to Me by your longings. I am not avoiding you; I am doing a work in you that is far deeper than what you see around you. I am drawing pain out of you—pain of longing, pain of rejection, and pain of feeling invisible to those from whom you wanted love. This pain is written upon the cells of your body. The pain needs to be released. I am drawing you deeper and deeper into a place that needs My love to fill it. Your time will come. Your life's experiences are yours alone, and the path you walk to Me will be different from any other. You are not too complicated to reach.

Trust Me when you do not see or hear. Trust the One who knows what you need. I do not withhold My love from you. My love is always with you. You perceive experiences as "My love" and as "lack of My love." In the spiritual realm, it is different. You will not always know what is happening. Trust Me with your heart. I will not hurt you; I will heal you. This is not meant to cause you grief, but to do My will in you. I am maturing you by not giving you all the experiences for which you long. This is the greater gift, that of maturing and delaying gratification. You need to be in love with your Lover and not just the gifts He gives you.

Do you love Me for Me, or for My gifts and for how you feel regarding them? Do you want growth and maturity, or do you want to be spoon-fed frequently? You cannot have both if you are to go where I want to take you. Choose the latter, and you will be a blessing. Go beyond the experience to the depth of union with Me. Believe in Me more than you believe in My gifts. I give My gifts to you, but you do not recognize that they are being worked into you. Some gifts will not be experienced as gifts.

Day 173: Whispering to the Cave of Your Heart

I will stand my watch
And set myself on the rampart,
And watch to see what He will say to me,
And what I will answer when I am corrected.
Habakkuk 2:1-2

...and after the earthquake a fire, but the Lord was not in the fire; and after the fire a still small voice.
1 Kings 19:12

Be still, and know that I am God;
I will be exalted among the nations,
I will be exalted in the earth!
Psalm 46:10

Dearest,

Hear Me in the silence. I beckon to you in the quiet. Come to your inner cave and wait. Listen for Me in faithfulness. Trust that I will be there to meet with My Beloved at our appointed time.

Come, My beloved Bride. Sit beside Me and listen. Listen and wait and believe. Am I not the faithful Bridegroom? Come to our meeting place. Place your trust and love in Me. Hear Me speak to your heart in our own silent language. The language that I speak to you is that of the Lover for the Beloved.

Come, My Beloved, My Bride. Sit and wait with Me and believe. Believe in the promises I give to you. Wed yourself to the promise to come to your cave to meet your Beloved in prayer. Meet Me in holy silence. Silence is the language of our love. Listen with your heart and you will hear. The heart has ears and believes. The heart responds in faithfulness. Come to Me in love. I wrap you in arms of eagerness. I welcome you to our inner cave. Will you come to Me and receive?

Day 174: Who Has Your Ear?

But you are a chosen generation, a royal priesthood, a holy nation, His own special people, that you may proclaim the praises of Him who called you out of darkness into His marvelous light...
1 Peter 2:9

...just as He chose us in Him before the foundation of the world, that we should be holy and without blame before Him in love, having predestined us to adoption as sons by Jesus Christ to Himself, according to the good pleasure of His will...
Ephesians 1:4-5

And you, being dead in your trespasses and the uncircumcision of your flesh, He has made alive together with Him, having forgiven you all trespasses, having wiped out the handwriting of requirements that was against us, which was contrary to us. And He has taken it out of the way, having nailed it to the cross.
Colossians 2:13-14

Dearest,

I will continue to develop your hearing of My voice. You sometimes forget that you are a temple of My Holy Spirit, and that I am present to you. Listen more, and I will tell you who you are and who I am. You have buried the truth of who you really are in Me, and you have listened to and believed the father of lies and his deceiving ways. Do not buy what he has whispered to you.

Stand back and receive the truth. Embrace the truth and release the lies.

Once you open the door to the truth, the lies must slink out the way they came in. Renew your mind with My Word. Enrich yourself in truth, and you will drown out all negative images and beliefs you previously held as truth.

Do not allow what someone tells you to change what I tell you. I do not tear down; I build up. Be discerning of the voices you entertain. Challenge that which is contrary to what I say.

Do not fear or be ashamed, as I am with you. I have made you equal to, not less than, others. Challenge those thoughts or words that come to rob you of your birthright. Stand up to those who would tear down My temple. Stand with Me, and be of good cheer, for I believe in you. I know what you are worth.

Day 175: You Are Anointed

Blessed is the nation whose God is the Lord,
The people He has chosen as His own inheritance.
Psalm 33:12

Blessed be the God and Father of our Lord Jesus Christ, who has blessed us with every spiritual blessing in the heavenly places in Christ, just as He chose us in Him before the foundation of the world, that we should be holy and without blame before Him in love...
Ephesians 1:3-4

For you are a holy people to the Lord your God, and the Lord has chosen you to be a people for Himself, a special treasure above all the peoples who are on the face of the earth.
Deuteronomy 14:2

My Beloved,

You are My Beloved. You have been called to show My love in this hurting world. You are not forgotten. Look and see how I have loved you. Do you not see My favor? I reach out to you with My love. Resist the lies of the enemy, and embrace the truth. You are anointed to serve. Your gifts are tailored to fit you. I do not give you lesser gifts. Can you trust Me even when you do not understand the whys? Reach out to others in love and see what I will do. Move from a place of waiting to a position of actively moving out of love and compassion. You do the reaching out. This is a new position for you. Your position has been one of waiting to be chosen, and I say that you already are chosen. Now go and choose others for My Kingdom.

Remove the goggles of past experiences. This is a new day. You are a new creation. Move to a position of being already chosen. Invite others in. Get off the bench in the waiting room. Keep moving in My Spirit. Do not wait for an invitation to come.

Day 176: You Do Not Need to Be a People-Pleaser

For do I now persuade men, or God?
Or do I seek to please men? For if I still pleased men, I would not be a bondservant of Christ.
Galatians 1:10

The fear of man brings a snare,
But whoever trusts in the Lord shall be safe.
Proverbs 29:25

Bondservants, obey in all things your masters according to the flesh, not with eyeservice, as men-pleasers, but in sincerity of heart, fearing God.
Colossians 3:22

Dearest One,

Come to Me, you who are weary, and I will give you rest. I will restore your soul, and I will renew you in My love. Come, stay awhile with Me. I can calm any storm. Trust your life to Me. I will calm you and set you in the right direction. Keep putting one foot in front of the other, and you will arrive where you need to be. You are not alone, and you are not helpless or less than others.

People can become angry with you, and it has nothing to do with you. Do not take on another's frustration, as this is not your job. You do not need to make everyone happy. Taking care of yourself may cause others to feel difficult feelings. Allow them to experience what is within them. Simply do what you need to do. You do not need to be forever pleasing to everyone you meet. Step away from this frustrating belief, as it is impossible to satisfy everyone. This is truth. Accept it—do not attempt the impossible. Why collect frustration?

Day 177: Your Healing Process

And be constantly renewed in the spirit of your mind [having a fresh mental and spiritual attitude], and put on the new nature (the regenerate self) created in God's image, [Godlike] in true righteousness and holiness.
Ephesians 4:23-24 AMP

You will guard him and keep him in perfect and constant peace whose mind [both its inclination and its character] is stayed on You, because he commits himself to You, leans on You, and hopes confidently in You.
Isaiah 26:3 AMP

You have turned my mourning into dancing for me; You have put off my sackcloth and girded me with gladness...
Psalm 30:11 AMP

Dearest One,

Hope is rising. Your time is coming—only believe. You are not too complicated to heal. My timing is perfect. Trust the One who knows you best to heal you. You, My child, have felt that you were a mystery that could never be solved. I am not perplexed by the mystery of your life. I know what to do and when to do it.

Be at peace, and leave the healing to Me. I will not leave you alone, and I am not forgetful. I see your frustrations at the timing of your healings. Things can change suddenly. You are not impossible for Me. I am

Lord and nothing is beyond My reach. I know where the walls are, and I can dismantle the walls.

Day 178: Discipline

But also for this very reason, giving all diligence, add to your faith virtue, to virtue knowledge, to knowledge self-control, to self-control perseverance, to perseverance godliness, to godliness brotherly kindness, and to brotherly kindness love. For if these things are yours and abound, you will be neither barren nor unfruitful in the knowledge of our Lord Jesus Christ.
2 Peter 1:5-8

Therefore we also, since we are surrounded by so great a cloud of witnesses, let us lay aside every weight, and the sin which so easily ensnares us, and let us run with endurance the race that is set before us, looking unto Jesus, the author and finisher of our faith, who for the joy that was set before Him endured the cross, despising the shame, and has sat down at the right hand of the throne of God.
Hebrews 12:1-2

Dear One,

Discipline is the means of receiving that which you seek. You must purpose yourself with intent in order to receive. You do not receive without first being open. Come into agreement with My purpose.

Am I not worth the effort to receive? Buffet yourself with discipline. Discipline is the means to that which you desire. Partner yourself with Me. Be willing to work for the prize. Was I not a model to follow? Do you want to be fully mature? Be willing to work. Am I worth your time?

Discipline is seen as distasteful in a fast-food culture. Are you willing to put in the time needed to be equipped in My Kingdom? Children do not need to work, but adults work by equipping themselves.

Clothe yourself in wisdom and truth from the fount of Life. Drink from the well of Salvation. Resist temptations, which are easy. Embrace the path of the cross. It is written that you may follow.

Day 179: Confidence

In the fear of the Lord there is strong confidence,
And His children will have a place of refuge.
Proverbs 14:26

...now the manifold wisdom of God might be made known by the church to the principalities and powers in the heavenly places, according to the eternal purpose which He accomplished in Christ Jesus our Lord, in whom we have boldness and access with confidence through faith in Him.
Ephesians 3:10-12

Therefore do not cast away your confidence, which has great reward.
Hebrews 10:35

Beloved,

I am He who names you. Does not the Creator know that which He created? I anointed you as royalty in My Kingdom. You are knighted with dignity and purpose. Value has been placed upon you.

You are touched and formed by My hands. I formed you for My specific plans and purposes. Will you have confidence in what has been placed within you? Do not settle for anything less than My Kingdom. Remain loyal to the King.

Live as one who is connected to My Holy Spirit. Remember who you are, and from whence you have come. Draw close to Me in anticipation of My speaking to you. Listen with faith, and not with fear.

Day 180: You Are My Friend

Greater love has no one than this, than to lay down one's life for his friends. You are My friends if you do whatever I command you. No longer do I call you servants, for a servant does not know what his master is doing; but I have called you friends, for all things that I heard from My Father I have made known to you.
John 15:13-15

He who calls you is faithful...
1 Thessalonians 5:24a

If we are faithless, He remains faithful;
He cannot deny Himself.
2 Timothy 2:13

Dearest,

My friendship with you is fierce. I am fiercely loyal to you. My love for you is eternal. I will lead you out of the thin places of belief to a broader place of faith.

You were meant for more, and you have settled for less. You have grazed on parched places, when I have lush meadows for you to feed upon. My child, come out of the land of less-than-enough. My Father owns the cattle on a thousand hills. Will He not share His wealth with you? I see you hiding and I am calling you out into the freedom of My love. Stand in My radiant presence. I do not call you to hide in the shadows of life. Come out, for I see you.

If you must hide, hide in the security of My love. I will teach you a new way of walking in My Kingdom. Be not afraid, for I am with you always.

Responses from the Bride

Day 181: Patricia's Psalm

Lord, You are my hope,
and You are worthy of my praise.
You, oh Lord, are my Friend,
and in You I seek refuge.
You will uplift me in times of darkness,
when in the nighttime of my pain,
morning seems never coming.
It is You alone, oh Lord,
who I must seek.
For You alone will lift my spirit,
and breathe life into me.
You know me, my Lord, as none other.
You search my heart and know my motives.
Your comfort and peace
is like sweet honey to the taste.
I long to rest in Your presence forever.
Never let me drift from Your friendship, oh God.
Help me to seek Your sweetness and mercy.
Remind me of who I am in You,
and that You alone can name me.
Hide me in the safety of Your love.
Imprint Your nature upon me.

You alone are worthy of all my love.
You will not keep me waiting at the altar.

Day 182: You Lifted Me

You lifted me from places of darkness.
You lifted me from places of being unknown.
You lifted me when I felt invisible.
You came, You saw, and now I am known.
You lifted me to the heart of the Father.
You came, and gave me a new family.
You moved across time and distance.
You lifted me from the lies of the enemy.
You revealed to me Your Word.
You lifted me into the heavenlies.
You lifted me to the throne of God.
You lifted me from the valley of my tears.
You came in love and made me whole.
You came and lifted me from a place of darkness.
You placed me in a place of love.
Your love melted all my sorrow.
You woke me up, that I may know Your love.
You lifted me to a place of freedom.
You lifted me to a place of love.

Day 183: Fear of the Lord

The Fear of the Lord is a person—awesome and majestic, wonderful and holy. The Fear of the Lord is powerful, and holds the power of life and death, blessing or a curse. Why would I choose sin over You? Knowing that You are with me, why would I offend You?

While The Fear of the Lord gives grace, there will also be judgment one day for my actions. In the presence of The Fear of the Lord, I am invited to change. My heart motives are stripped away in Your glory. Do I dare hold onto sin, when You invite me to choose love in its place? Who am I to insist on petty behaviors of this world, when I could stand before You in Your glorious presence?

The Fear of the Lord invites me to better choices and a higher way of living. In Your presence, all I want to do is to worship You. Everything else falls away, and I am struck by reverence and honor toward You.

Lord Jesus, strip me of all unrighteous desires and actions. Purify my motives until they are as pure as Love Himself. Open my eyes to Your wonder and truth. I want to embrace what You embrace. Write Your nature upon the tablet of my heart.

Help me not to settle for the world, when I can be in Your presence. In Your presence, I want to lie prostrate before You. Oh, Holy One of Israel, You came to teach me. Teach me all that I need to know, dearest Lord. I pray for the grace to stand in the Refiner's Fire. Your methods produce the results that You desire. Amen.

Day 184: Reverence

To fear You, Lord, is to hold You in a place of honor and reverence. To fear the Lord is to pay attention to what You say and do. I do not want to take for granted who You are. You are my Friend, and that is a privilege.

Help me, Lord, to put You in a place of highest importance in my life, and not in an "if there is time for You" place. You are the glory of God come to earth. How do I comprehend You, my Lord? How does deity come down to us, my Lord? I do not want to be irreverent toward You.

How do I befriend royalty? It all feels so confusing, so difficult for my mind to comprehend. As deity, you seem far away. As God's son, Jesus, come to humble circumstances, I can come closer. It is so complex for me, Lord, to understand who You are, and what You have done for me. Teach me reverence in order to honor You. Help me to run to the throne and not slink away. King of Glory, You came down to us. What a great love, indeed.

Day 185: Word of God

You are Jesus, Word of God.
All truth is found in You.
Teach me truth, as You are Truth,
that I may know You fully,
oh Wisdom of the Ages.
Oh, One of beauty and truth,
give me revelation
from the heart of Heaven itself.
In understanding and knowledge
there is freedom.
Set me free from the lies that deceive,
that I may stand with you in truth.
Oh Holy Wisdom of God,
draw me closer to the throne of God.
Your words are life.
They are sharper than a two-edged sword.
Illuminate for me,
that I may see and stand in wonder
and awe of the One who speaks
from Heaven's throne.
Oh Beautiful One, oh Ancient of Days,
release your words from Heaven.

Help me to dwell in Your presence.
Hide me in the safety of Your truth.
No lie can be found in You.
Wisdom of the Ages,
speak to me of Your knowledge.
You are holy,
and I stand in awe of You.
Oh, Wonder of Wonders,
I have access to Your throne.
How blessed am I to have revelation and understanding.
No other King is as approachable as You.
Beautiful One, I desire to bask in Your glory.
Oh, Wonder of Heaven,
You come close to those
who call upon Your holy name.
Walk with me, I pray,
that Your knowledge and understanding
may fall upon me.
You, oh Lord, are the Teacher,
and I am your student.
Help me to glean from Your teachings.
I am standing with You upon holy ground,
in this, our classroom.

Gather me to You,
as a mother hen does her chicks.
Let me drink in the fullness of Your wisdom.
Oh, Shepherd of God, Your lamb is waiting.
Lead me to Your pools of knowledge.
I need to drink freely,
and to rest in Your presence.
You alone can quench my thirst.

Day 186: Confidence

I was born as a daughter of a King. Dare I live as less than my birthright? I am called, named, and purposed. How does royalty live? I live in knowing and not in denial. I belong to One who is greater. Just knowing this is humbling indeed.

Oh seed of greatness, I will rise up to the value of the One who values me. I will rise as the noble one He calls me to be and walk in dignity, for His blood runs in my veins. I will not settle for less than that for which I was created.

I am a filled vessel, not one that is abandoned. The Spirit of the living God resides in me. He is alive and not dormant. He hears my every prayer. Will He not respond in kind to me? I am empowered by the Lord Almighty. As the tabernacle of Your Holy Spirit, I will walk with You as You lead me. You listen and speak within.

Day 187: Determination

Oh, pillar of strength and power,
You determine to press on toward the goal.
Nothing can change Your focus.
Your eyes are on the prize.
Fix in me that focus.
Set my heart upon You and Your call.
Stretch me to reach new arenas of faith.
You are the Prize that I seek.
Help me to shake off the distractions
that get in my way.
Break off of me the fear that entangles.
Press on in me through the walls of doubt.
Let me not stop here and camp
in the Land of Limitations.
Help me to press on to
the Promised Land within me.
I am no longer a prisoner of my past.
Let me not be content to live in the Land of Less,
when You have abundance for me.
It is Your footsteps that I must follow.
Lead me.

Day 188: Knowing

In the overshadowing of the Holy Spirit, I am impregnated with the Spirit. The Spirit visits me in the nighttime of my life. Come, Holy Spirit, visit me with Your presence. Bring life into my barren womb, that I may enter into a union of knowing You intimately, as You know me intimately. Wake me up to Your presence. I surrender to Your touch. In You I am awakened to truth.

All-knowing Spirit of God, fill me with Your presence. I want to be wed to You. You alone know who I am. Place and stir within me all that you desire.

This is indeed holy ground, as I am one with You. Help me to know my identity as a temple of the Holy Spirit. Sing songs of deliverance over me, that I may be set free to say my yes to You.

Day 189: Desire

Oh, flame of life within me,
Embers sparked by divine union—
Fan into flame the desire for life in the Holy Spirit.
Wash over me from above and within me.
Stir up the willingness to be filled with my purpose.
I want to move in the anointing of Your presence.
Move in me.
Lead me in a dance of obedience and fulfillment.
You must lead and I must follow.
Lead me all the way back home.

Day 190: You Are Holy

Oh, Lord, You are holy indeed.
I stand in awe of Your presence.
How honored am I
that the Holy One of God
should know my name.
Name above all names,
You call me friend.
How do I receive such a gift of love
from Love Himself?
How do I love You in return
for Your fierce love?
You are a Friend
who is closer than a brother.
Oh, Radiant One, who sees all things,
teach me how to be Your friend.
I do not deserve a love such as Yours.
Yet, I will not turn it down.
Oh, One who knows no sin,
teach me how to live my life.
I want to bring joy to Your heart.
Please help me to not cause You grief.
Beloved of God, look into my heart.

Remove whatever displeases You.
You are the Jewel of the Father, Jesus,
the Priceless One.
Hold me close, my Friend,
and never let me go.
I want to lie in Your arms,
like Your friend John did.
You found friendship with John;
please also find a friend in me.
This is bold indeed to think
that I could rest in Your arms.
Come closer, my Friend.
My life is lonely without You.
You bring joy to my soul.
You, Lord, are the keeper of my secrets.
I trust You to not expose my heart to man.
Mold me into one of Your liking.
Who am I, to have You as my Friend?
Heaven came to a stable and gave birth.
You changed the stable of my heart
into a palace when You entered it.
You are the God who comes near.
Oh, Radiant Love of the Father,
Mercy and Grace Himself,
be glorified this day.

Be exalted, King of Kings,
my forever Friend, for all seasons.
Oh, Jesus, You have my back.
You will not let me fall.
You know my every tear—
not one is lost to You.
Lord, You do not sleep or grow weary.
Strengthen me by Your love.
Rose of Sharon, Lilly of the Valley,
Your fragrance is sweet indeed.
I want to be like Mary and sit at Your feet.
I want to break open the alabaster box of my heart
and pour a sweet fragrance of love over You.

Day 191: Purpose

You have placed Your purpose within me, like a gift under a Christmas tree. From the beginning of time, You saw me. "This is who she is," You said. You formed me with purpose and destiny. I am carved with a set purpose.

Oh, wonderful One, who designs all life, direct me. Show me the path to follow. Can I be anything less than intended? Dare I attempt to recreate another? I am tailored to fit Your purpose for me. Help me to submit and to follow You.

Direct me, that I follow Your plans alone. I am made for You alone in this season of time. For such a time as this was I purposed. Fashion me as You intended. Keep me close to You, my God. Do not let me get lost on this journey.

Day 192: My Identity

This is a new day. That which held life and death is no more. I will step into this new day that You have made. I will rejoice, for I have passed over from one day to another new day. I will say farewell to what once was, and embrace this new season of promises and possibilities.

I have yet to see this new direction in the land that I am entering, but when I cannot see where I am going, I will listen for Your voice. You will lead me through the wilderness. Even in the desert, You will provide rivers of nourishment to quench my thirst for You. I will stay close to You so I will not lose my way. You are the Way Maker.

Is anything beyond Your reach? You see from the beginning of time to the present day, and beyond to the future. I will step into Your daily provision. I will trust the One who calls me, for You are the Trustworthy One. I will embrace You.

You call me a filled vessel, not one that is abandoned. The Spirit of the living God resides in me, and He is alive and not dormant. You hear my every prayer. Will You not respond in kind to me?

I am empowered by the Lord Almighty. I am the tabernacle of Your Holy Spirit, and I will walk with You as You lead me. I listen and You speak within me. Could You do any less than this?

Day 193: My Prayer

Oh, creative Father God,
In You is all possibility and potential.
You are limitless.
Nothing can contain what is possible for You.
You are without borders.
Come to me and change my vision and my expectations.
I want to be open to see and to hear You.
Where I am blind, Lord, let me see.
Where I am deaf,
open my spiritual ears to Your voice within.
You know my limitations.
I want to step into Your unfolding plan for my life.
Surprise me by Your goodness.
Wake me up to my potential.
Create in me the creativity of my Father.
Express through me Your unfolding message.
You are the Author and I am Your pen.

Day 194: Gratitude

Oh, God of wonder and might—
You are the God who comes near.
You know the desires of my heart, and You heard me,
one of many in the universe.
Oh God, my Father, You answered my heart's cry.
Prayers heard, prayers answered from a depth of longing.
You, too, long for me to come and be with You.
Your longing and waiting are in my hands,
as I decide how busy I am this day.
Yet, the God of the universe is waiting,
waiting for His Beloved to come closer.
Who am I to run in circles,
being busy and scattered by things to do,
or with distractions that are enticing?
And, He waits for me,
much more patiently than I wait for Him.
He waits in peace, as He is Peace.
Why do I keep You waiting,
when You are the One who is so great?
What an honor it is that You wait for me.
How do I thank You for everything?

I am indeed grateful, my Father, and Provider.
How generous You are, indeed.
Am I not wealthy in blessings given?
Are You not the Giver of all good gifts?
You notice, and when I notice, You smile.
"She sees," You say, as One who is so wise,
When even seeing is a gift given by the
Almighty Benefactor and Lover of my soul.
You are kind and merciful,
and I bow down in gratitude that You love me.
Oh, Giver of all good things,
I offer You my humble gratitude, wrapped in love.
Please receive this from Your child,
who seeks to honor You this day.
I see You with me, and You are good.
Grace and Mercy met this day indeed. Amen.

Day 195: My Thoughts

My thoughts have wandered from my true home
to that of a foreign land.
I listen to one who holds no truth in him.
He has wrapped his lies in a kernel of truth
or tantalizing lie.
Why do my ears perk up when he whispers lies
to trap me in a snare?
Have I so quickly lost my way,
that I would allow a stranger,
who has lost his way, to direct me?
My navigation must be reset by the Word of God.
It is written, that I may believe.
It is written, that I may recognize truth.
Truth from Truth Himself
is the direction and the way home.
Align me once more, my Lord,
that I fix my eyes upon the good,
that I may see and recognize once more
that which is before me.
Help me to cleanse my temple,
so that it is fit for you to dwell within.

Holiness is what I long for.

Holiness is what I choose.

Help me to be selective of what I listen to,

and of what speaks to me.

Help me to move quickly past the lies that ensnare,

and swift to embrace truth.

May I partner with your loving words—words of life to set me free.

Made in the USA
Charleston, SC
28 February 2015